THE CIVILIZED
SHOPPER'S GUIDE TO
FLORENCE

THE CIVILIZED SHOPPER'S GUIDE

to Florence

LOUISE FILI

The Little Bookroom • New York

Research assistance: Lise Apatoff
Photographs © 2007 by Louise Fili
Book design: Louise Fili Ltd
Maps: Todd Pasini

Library of Congress Cataloging-in-Publication Data
Fili, Louise.
The civilized shopper's guide to Florence / by Louise Fili.
p. cm.
Includes index.
ISBN 1-892145-47-2 (alk. paper)
1. Shopping—Italy—Florence—Guidebooks.
2. Florence (Italy)—Guidebooks. I. Title.
TX337.I82F55 2007
381'.1094551—dc22
2007002473

Published by The Little Bookroom
435 Hudson Street, 3rd Floor
New York, NY 10014
(212) 293-1643
fax (212) 333-5374
editorial@littlebookroom.com
www.littlebookroom.com

Printed in China
Second Printing

TABLE OF CONTENTS

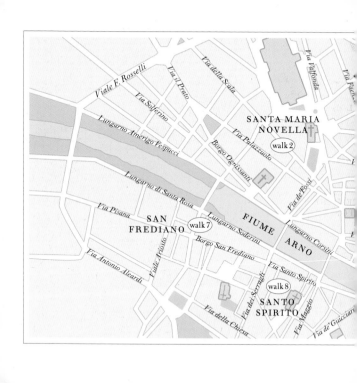

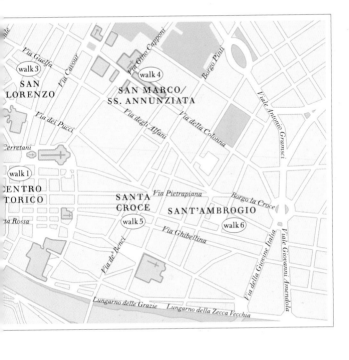

INTRODUCTION

WHILE FLORENTINES BEMOAN THE INFLUX OF THE MEGA DESIGNER STORES THAT FURTHER globalize their beautiful city, it is nonetheless impressive to see how many family businesses—milliners, bookstores, art supply shops, bakeries, woodcarvers, silversmiths—have continued to flourish for generations.

For Gabriele and Gherardo Filistrucchi, whose eponymous shop creates custom wigs, it is business as usual since 1720—same name, same building, and two floods later. Or consider artisans like Simone Taddei, who learned the 32-step process of making leather-covered boxes from his father and grandfather—or Ilaria Ballatresi of Dolci & Dolcezze whose sublime flourless chocolate cake has for decades drawn devotees worldwide.

Whether it is a multi-generational enterprise, or young entrepreneurs who offer a new interpretation of traditional techniques, all share a commitment to excellence using time-honored techniques, which is what *The Civilized Shopper's Guide to Florence* seeks to celebrate.

This book is divided into eight walks, although one of the biggest pleasures of Florence is wandering the winding streets and making your own discoveries. As all exploration requires sustenance, favorite restaurants, cafés, wine bars and gelaterias are listed at the conclusion of each section. *Buon divertimento!*

LEGEND

(1) SHOPS (A) FOOD & DRINK

▭ ACCEPTS CREDIT CARDS

⧸ DOES NOT ACCEPT CREDIT CARDS

SOME PRACTICAL INFORMATION

HOURS: Most shops in Florence are open from 9 or 10am to 1pm, and 3:30-7:30pm, though some remain open all day. In autumn, winter, and spring, shops are closed on Monday mornings; in summer (June 15 through the end of August), they close instead on Saturday afternoons. For the purposes of this book, "winter" hours are listed. (Since most shops are closed all or part of August, summer hours are short-lived.) Few shops are open on Sunday, whatever the season.

CHIUSO: Possibly the saddest word in the Italian language, this often appears on shop doors at unanticipated times, and means, simply, *closed*. It can be an indication of a momentary inconvenience, or, when paired with *per sciopero* (strike), it can last the day. (*Torno subito*—back soon—is more hopeful.) Don't despair; by changing course a few degrees you'll undoubtedly stumble onto something equally wonderful elsewhere.

HOLIDAYS: The city comes to a virtual halt on these religious and state holidays: January 1, January 6, Easter Sunday and Monday, April 25, May 1, June 24, August 15, November 1, December 8, December 25 and 26. Keep in mind that bus service will be discontinued, although Florence is a delight to explore *a piedi*.

CREDIT CARDS: Many of the shops listed in this book take credit cards, although very few accept American Express. Plan accordingly.

RESTAURANT RESERVATIONS: Although lunch without a reservation is usually not a problem (assuming you arrive by 1:00pm), a *prenotazione* is recommended for dinner. While it was once a challenge to dine out on a Sunday in Florence, more and more restaurants are now staying open seven days a week.

SHOPPING ETIQUETTE: Even if you don't have a command of their language, most Italians will appreciate any attempt at communication, no matter how badly you mangle *"Buon giorno, Signora (Signore)"* when entering a shop. Always say thank you when leaving: *"Grazie, Signora (Signore). Buon giorno"* (used in the morning); *"Buona sera"* (anytime from the afternoon on).

THE DE MEDICI CODE

DURING THE *RISORGIMENTO*, OR "RESURGENCE," THE POLITICAL AND SOCIAL PROCESS THAT UNIfied Italy during the nineteenth century, the city of Florence experienced massive urban renewal. It had become apparent that businesses that were once simply people selling from carts, market stalls, or out of ground floors of family homes, were now evolving into the kinds of operations we know today—large and small shops separate from street and home. This posed a distinct municipal problem: how to distinguish business from home addresses. Since it would have been impossible to renumber the entire city, a unique numbering classification was born. As a result, to the dismay and confusion of today's visitors, buildings in Florence operate on two numbering systems. Buildings housing commercial businesses have red numbers, mean-

[14]

ing that the number listed in the address is followed by an r for *rosso*. The red number on the facade of the building tends to be engraved into a square marble slab, and, with age, appears to be anything but red.

Residential numbers are written with (or without) an n for *nero* (black), even though the numbers on the buildings are actually blue, on a white ceramic plate.

While the addresses in this guide are shops and hence should be red, this is not always the case. The red and black numbers do not necessarily correspond (i.e., number 57r can be directly across the street from, say, 100r, and next to 31n). Moreover, examples of "red" numbers styled in black (see two bottom photos at left), and vice-versa, are apt to crop up every now and then.

When all else fails, consult the map at the beginning of each walk. Should you become completely frustrated, a stop at a *gelateria* or wine bar (also indicated on the map) is a highly recommended diversion.

WALK 1 ◆ CENTRO STORICO

Piazza del Duomo

Via del Campidoglio

Via Brunelleschi

Via de' Tosinghi

Via Roma

Via de' Medici

Via de' Calzaiuoli

Via delle Oche

Via Santa Elisabetta

Via dello Studio

Via del Proconsolo

Piazza della Republica

Via degli Strozzi

Via Spezlali

Via del Corso

Via de' Pec[ori]

Via de' Sassetti

Via de' Pellicceria

Via Calimala

Via dei Tavolini

Via dei Cerchi

Via Santa Margherita

Via del Presto

Via Dante Alighieri

Badia

Via dei Lamberti

Via dei Cimatori

Via della Condotta

Piazza San Firenze

Via Porta Rossa

Via Calimaruzza

Via del Bombarde

Via del Fiordaliso

Via del Terme

Via Calimaruzza

Via Vaccherreccia

Piazza della Signoria

Via del Gondi

Corso de' Tintori

Borgo SS. Apostoli

Via Por Santa Maria

Palazzo Vecchio

Via Lambertesca

Corso de' Baroncelli

Via dei Leoni

E 8 10 6 7 D 9 5 4 C 2 B 3 A 11 12 13 1

SHOPS

1. Laura Nutini
2. Tharros Bijoux
3. Bizzarri
4. Taddei
5. Zecchi
6. Pegna
7. Paperback Exchange
8. Nante
9. Samba Mercerie
10. Rosa Regale
11. Passamaneria Valmar
12. Infinity
13. Simone Abbarchi

FOOD & DRINK

A. Rivoire
B. Caffè Italiano
C. I Fratellini
D. Coquinarius
E. Gelateria Grom

LAURA NUTINI

VIA LAMBERTESCA 8R

▭ ☎ 055 2396563

MON 3:30-7PM; TUE-SAT 9:30AM-1PM & 3:30-7PM

CLOSED SUNDAY

FOR EXQUISITE HANDMADE LINENS, NIGHT-GOWNS, LINGERIE, AND HANDKERCHIEFS *"PER signora/bambina/casa,"* as her business card reads, look no further than Laura Nutini.

Over the course of decades, the owner has assembled a group of expert seamstresses who produce handmade, one-of-a-kind creations in the classical tradition.

Signora Nutini proudly shows a gossamer, hand-embroidered nightgown that a customer found so enchanting, she chose to wear it as a wedding dress.

Astonishingly beautiful hand-sewn monograms are a must-see, and are available in a variety of styles.

[19]

THARROS BIJOUX

VIA DELLA CONDOTTA,
CORNER OF VICOLO DE' CERCHI 2R
▭ ☎ 055 284126 · *www.tharros.com*
MON-SAT 10AM-1PM & 3:30-7:30PM
CLOSED SUNDAY

IF YOU EVER HAD A SECRET DESIRE TO DRESS LIKE ELEANORA OF TOLEDO IN HER FAMOUS PORTRAIT by Bronzino, head straight to Tharros Bijoux.

This small, beautiful shop tucked into Via della Condotta showcases jewelry designs inspired by Renaissance paintings. Working with garnets, amethysts, emeralds, sapphires, rubies, and lapis lazuli, Carlo Amato creates dazzling museum reproductions of necklaces, earrings, bracelets, pendants, rings, and brooches that are royalty-worthy, yet very affordably priced.

[21]

BIZZARRI

VIA DELLA CONDOTTA 32R

✆ 055 211580

MON-FRI 9:30AM-1PM & 4-7:30PM; SAT 9:30AM-1PM

CLOSED SUNDAY & AUGUST

ALTHOUGH BIZZARRI SEEMS LIKE AN APT NAME FOR THIS QUIRKY SHOP OF VAGUELY MYSTERIOUS glass-fronted dark wood cabinets, it is in fact named after its nineteenth-century founder, Dottor Alessandro Bizzarri. Once inside, you will be mesmerized by the array of test tubes and apothecary jars, with neatly typed labels, of spices, extracts, essences, and herbal elixirs. Ask for an *estratto* (extract) of anything from acacia to *zenzero* (ginger) and watch as it is aspirated from a jar using a large calibrated glass straw, then deposited into a tiny glass bottle with an affixed handwritten label. This experience alone is well worth the visit.

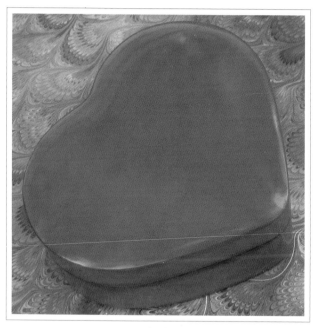

[24]

TADDEI

VIA SANTA MARGHERITA 11

▭ ☎ 055 2398960

MON-SAT 8AM-8PM

CLOSED SUNDAY & AUGUST

HIDDEN AWAY ON A TINY STREET ACROSS FROM CASA DI DANTE IS THE WORKSHOP OF THE extraordinary artisan Simone Taddei. In the tradition of his father and grandfather, Taddei makes exquisite, highly polished leather boxes in a myriad of sizes and forms. Working completely alone, Taddei first makes a wooden mold, which is then sanded, covered in calfskin, and stained in a selection of rich colors. From small coin purses to elaborate Louis XIV chests of drawers, Taddei can't ever seem to produce fast enough: *"Questa roba vola dal negozio,"* he sighs, barely looking up from his work table. ("This stuff flies out of the store.")

ZECCHI

VIA DELLO STUDIO 19R

☎ 055 211470 · *www.zecchi.com*

MON 3:30-7:30PM; TUE-SAT 8:30AM-12:30PM &

3:30-7:30PM; CLOSED SUNDAY & AUGUST

THERE'S A GOOD CHANCE THAT ANY RESTORATION WORK IN FLORENCE—OR THROUGHOUT the world, for that matter—has been done using materials from this renowned art supply store. Zecchi carries a dazzling array of the same beautifully colored dry pigments, gilding supplies, hand-forged sculpture tools, and paintbrushes that were used by Renaissance masters. For the more modern-minded artist, a full line of Zecchi's own acrylics, pastels, and colored pencils is also available. Don't miss the *tavolozze per i mancini*—wooden palettes crafted for the left-handed painter, or *camicie del pittore*—classic smocks for the artist or restorer.

PEGNA

VIA DELLO STUDIO 8

▭ ☎ 055 282701 · *www.pegna.it*

MON-SAT 9AM-1PM & 3:30-7:30PM

CLOSED WEDNESDAY PM AND SUNDAY

IT WOULDN'T BE FAIR TO CALL PEGNA A SUPER-MARKET. JUST STEPS FROM THE DUOMO, THIS grand *drogheria/mesticheria/salumeria*, as the sign proclaims, has been serving Florentines and tourists alike since 1860. Don't be fooled by the display of toothbrushes and floor cleaners as you enter; as the store unfolds, an elegant array of international and organic products, from paté to fine chocolates, comes into view. The *salumeria* has excellent prepared foods that will ensure that your last supper—on the plane going home—will be a memorable one. The cheerful, green-jacketed staff will help you with your purchases, which can be delivered.

PAPERBACK EXCHANGE

VIA DELLE OCHE 4R

▭ ☎ 055 293460 · *www.papex.it*

MON-FRI 9AM-7:30PM; SAT 10AM-1PM & 3:30-7:30PM

CLOSED SUNDAY

BILLING THEMSELVES AS THE "ANGLO-AMERICAN BOOKSHOP," PAPERBACK EXCHANGE HAS BEEN A fixture in the English-speaking community since 1979, when Maurizio Panichi and Emily Rosner first opened their doors. Now relocated in an airy space in the Centro Storico, this shop is the source for thousands of titles in English, many relating to Italy (or more specifically to Florence). The helpful staff can order any book from the US or UK within 2-3 working days. As their name implies, Paperback Exchange also buys secondhand books, at reasonable prices. Author readings and community-related events are scheduled on a regular basis.

NANTE

PIAZZA DEL DUOMO 52R

✆ 055 2396002

MON-SAT 9AM-12PM; CLOSED SUNDAY

THIS SIGN STORE FACING THE DUOMO HAS BEEN IN OPERATION SINCE 1879, WHICH IS QUITE POS-sibly the last time the window was washed. Proprietor Mario Nante, grandson of the founder, supplies Florentines with *targhe*—enamel plaques—of every variety: house numbers, WC, *toilette*, *cucina*, *vietato fumare* (no smoking—if only Signor Nante would comply!). Custom signs can be ordered and sent to you.

Nante is open most mornings, but as for the afternoons, he shrugs, *"Dipende dall'umore"* (Depending on my mood). Although he is quick to inform you that he doesn't speak English, if there ever were a time for sign language, this is it.

[33]

SAMBA MERCERIE

VIA SANTA ELISABETTA 10R

≠ ☎ 055 215193

MON 3:30-6:30PM;

TUE-SAT 9AM-12:30PM & 3:30-6:30PM

CLOSED SUNDAY

BEHIND THE UNASSUMING FACADE OF THIS 70-YEAR-OLD SHOP IS AN IMPOSING WALL OF buttons in every conceivable color, style, and material, all carefully arranged by hue. While owner Marco Scilla can't begin to estimate the number of *bottoni* in his inventory, he does know that they are *"novanta-nove per cento italiani."* Scilla's patience with his customers is legendary. No matter how many people are crowded into the shop (taking a number is advised), he will spend whatever time is necessary to guarantee that you go home with just the right button.

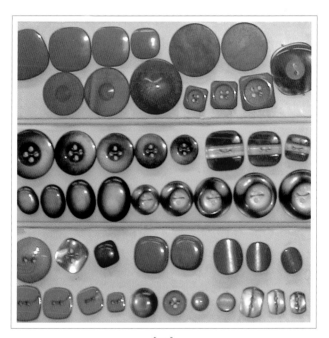

[35]

[36]

ROSA REGALE

VIA DE'TOSINGHI, VOLTA MAZZUCCONI 3R

☎ 055 2670613 · *www.rosaregale.it*

MON 3:30-7:30PM; TUE-SAT 10AM-1PM & 3-7:30PM

CLOSED SUNDAY

FROM VIA DE'TOSINGHI, FOLLOW THE VAULTED PASSAGEWAY ADORNED WITH FLORENTINE CRESTS into this enchanting shop, where the subject is not just roses, but all flower motifs.

From fanciful, opulent red velvet chairs and ottomans to dresses, jewelry, and handbags, the floral theme makes its way throughout Rosa Regale. The upholstered seats for pets are especially charming, as are the elegant and unusual tie-backs, pillows, and table lamps.

Not surprisingly, the shop clerk will write up your order with a flower-adorned pen.

PASSAMANERIA VALMAR

VIA PORTA ROSSA 53R

☎ 055 284493 · *www.valmar-florence.com*

MON-FRI 9AM-7:30PM; SAT 10AM-7:30PM

CLOSED SUNDAY

SINCE THE 1960S, THIS QUINTESSENTIALLY FLOR-ENTINE, HYPER-ELEGANT TRIMMINGS SHOP HAS been the place for nobility (or their servants) to buy classic *nappe*, or *fiocchi* (tassels), decorative pillows and buttons, tie backs, ribbons, edging, tablecloths and runners, all in a rich palette of Renaissance colors.

Valmar features intricate appliqués of Florentine crests for pillows or curtains, which for years have been handmade with antique fabrics by the same seamstress. *"Dopo di lei è la fine. Nessuno sa come farlo,"* the owner says wistfully. (After she's gone will be the end. No one else knows how to make them anymore.)

[40]

INFINITY

BORGO SS. APOSTOLI 18R

▭ ☎ 055 2398405 · *infinityfirenze.com*

MON 2:30-7PM; TUE-SAT 10AM-1PM & 2:30-7PM

CLOSED SUNDAY & AUGUST

FOR MORE THAN 20 YEARS, EUGENIO PROVARONI AND HIS AMERICAN WIFE, JANE, HAVE BEEN crafting distinctive handmade leather purses, belts, and wallets in their workshop on Borgo SS. Apostoli.

Drawing from a vast selection of leathers—calf, cowhide, sheepskin, suede, fur, deer, elk, snakeskin, alligator, and crocodile—their creations range from classic to more contemporary styles.

Choose from hundreds of styles of buckles, and they will make any size and color belt while you wait. Handbags can be made to your specifications (they will happily add that extra zipper or inner pocket) in one week.

SIMONE ABBARCHI

BORGO SS. APOSTOLI 16

☎ 055 210552

MON 3:30-7:30PM; TUE-SAT 10:30AM-1PM &
3:30-7:30PM; CLOSED SUNDAY & AUGUST

IN HIS ELEGANT SHOP NEAR THE PIAZZA SANTA TRINITA, SIMONE ABBARCHI MAKES EXQUISITELY tailored handmade shirts for men and women, as well as suits, jackets, pants, and ties, all to order.

Ranging from the traditional man's dress shirt to cotton and linen trousers in extravagant shades of saffron and watermelon, all are produced in his Fiesole workshop. Allow one month for your order, which can be shipped worldwide.

The very helpful staff speaks English.

Note that this address has a black, not red, number.

WALK 1 ✦ FOOD & DRINK

(A)

RIVOIRE
Piazza della Signoria 5 🔲 ☎ 055 214412
8am-midnight, closed Monday · Moderate

Enjoy sublime hot chocolate while taking in the Palazzo Vecchio.

(B)

CAFFÈ ITALIANO
Via della Condotta 56r 🚫 ☎ 055 291082
Mon-Fri 8:15am-8pm; Sat 8:15am-9pm; Sun 8:15am-11pm
Moderate

The charming, old-world Caffè Italiano is a good option for a lei-
surely light lunch. Sit upstairs and choose from a selection of salads,
crostini, panini, and *pizzette*, or just unwind with a cup of their
excellent coffee. Try the "*caffè-ciok*," the best thing to ever happen
to espresso, hot chocolate, and steamed milk.

(C)

I FRATELLINI
Via dei Cimatori 38r 🚫 ☎ 055 2396096
8am-8pm, closed Sunday · Inexpensive

When the awning is down, there is no evidence of their name;
just look for a lively crowd standing in the street eating happily.
I Fratellini serves fresh, delicious panini, out of this literal hole

in the wall, in twenty-seven different varieties. A sandwich and a glass of decent Chianti will set you back only a few euros. Roman numerals marked on wooden shelves on the exterior wall will help you locate your glass after you set it down.

COQUINARIUS
Via delle Oche 15r 🖃 ☎ 055 2302153
Sun-Thu 12-11pm; Fri-Sat 12-11:30pm, closed August · Moderate
This very comfortable wine bar is ideal for a light meal at just about any time of the day. Eighteen kinds of salads (many of which are vegetarian) are on the menu, as well as crostini, unusual ravioli, and a good selection of wines by the glass. Very friendly service.

GELATERIA GROM
Via del Campanile 2 (at Via delle Oche)
🚫 ☎ 055 216158 · *www.grom.it*
Daily 10:30am-11:30pm · Moderate
Their motto, "*Il gelato come una volta,*" (Gelato the way it used to be) speaks volumes. Choosing only fresh, seasonal ingredients of the highest quality (strawberries in summer, oranges in winter; lemons and pistachios from Sicily), Grom serves up excellent, albeit somewhat pricey, gelato that is well worth every euro.

WALK 2 ✦ SANTA MARIA NOVELLA

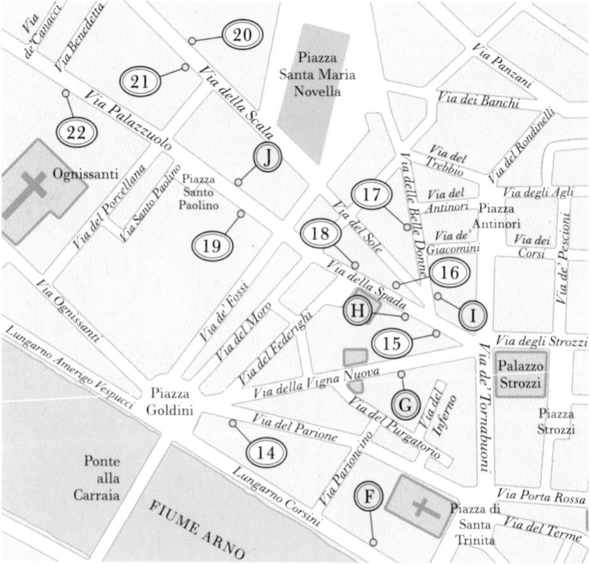

SHOPS

(14) Elio Ferraro

(15) Grevi

(16) Assolibri

(17) Ugo e Carolina

(18) Tip Tap

(19) Quisquilia e Pinzillacchera

(20) Officina Profumo Farmaceutica di Santa Maria Novella

(21) Dolceforte

(22) Bronzista Baldini

FOOD & DRINK

(F) Capocaccia

(G) Caffè Amerini

(H) Marione

(I) Osteria Belle Donne

(J) Amon

ELIO FERRARO

VIA DEL PARIONE 47R

📠 ☎ 055 290425 · *www.elioferraro.com*

MON-SAT 9:30AM-7:30PM; CLOSED SUNDAY

E LIO FERRARO'S EPONYMOUS SHOP IS AN EXCEL-
LENT RESOURCE FOR VINTAGE FRENCH AND
Italian designer clothing and accessories from the twenties through the nineties; on any given day you will find a Puccini, Missoni, Cardin, Chanel, Hermès, or Courrèges original.

The shop is a period piece in itself—a lively and eclectic mix of clothes, shoes, and accessories juxtaposed with designer furniture—tables, lamps, and vases from such innovators as Sottssas, Fornasetti, Ponti, and Colombo.

Ferraro's museum-worthy collection of handbags—a tour-de-force of every imaginable period and style—is not to be missed.

[49]

15

GREVI

VIA DELLA SPADA 11/13R

▭ ☎ 055 264139 · *www.grevi.com*

MON-SAT 10AM-8PM;

OPEN THE LAST SUNDAY OF THE MONTH

T HIS TINY, FOURTH-GENERATION *CAPPELLERIA* IS A CELEBRATION OF STYLISH HATS FOR MEN, women, and children, all made by hand in Grevi's nearby workshop. Wool, felt, velvet, straw, organza, and cotton are expertly crafted with fanciful flowers, appliqués, and embroidery into delicious works of art in a spectrum of colors. The *scarpine* (little shoes) and gloves for children are hard to resist. Equally delightful handbags and fans are also available.

The friendly staff speaks English and will be happy to ship your purchases for you.

[51]

16

ASSOLIBRI

VIA DEL SOLE 3R

▬ ☎ 055 284533

MON 3:30-7:30PM; TUE-SAT 10:15AM-2PM,
3:30-7:30PM; CLOSED SUNDAY

IN THIS BRIGHT, MODERN SPACE AT THE NEXUS OF VIA DEL SOLE AND VIA DELLA SPADA, OVER-sized books and periodicals on the subject of fine art, graphic design, architecture, photography, and fashion coexist with an ever-changing art exhibition. Italian and European publishers are well represented, and some of the books are in English.

Posters and postcards are also available, and browsing is encouraged.

[53]

[54]

UGO E CAROLINA

VIA DELLE BELLE DONNE 35R

☎ 055 287820

MON 3-7PM; TUE-SAT 9:30AM-1PM & 2:30-7PM

CLOSED SUNDAY

PROPRIETORS CATIA AND LUCIA JOINED FORCES NEARLY TWO DECADES AGO WITH A SINGLE MIS-sion: to dress Florentine children even more impeccably than their mothers. As a result of their efforts, Ugo e Carolina has enjoyed a reputation for clothing *bambini* in exquisite style, carrying only the best of Italian and European labels: Le Nouveau Né, Seeds, Marni, Frigerio, Lola Parker, and Nicoletta Fanna.

The gracious staff will help you select from clothes, shoes, hats, and socks for newborns to age sixteen. Choose from royalty-worthy christening gowns to accessories for expectant and new mothers, all in incomparable taste.

TIP TAP

VIA DELLA SPADA 50R

▭ ☎ 055 2398488

MON 3:30-7:30PM;

TUE-SAT 10AM-1PM & 3:30-7:30PM; CLOSED SUNDAY

TIP TAP KEEPS THE FEET OF LOCAL *BAMBINI* IN STYLE FROM BIRTH TO SIZE NINE (WHICH means that some lucky grown-ups can shop here as well.) Every pair of beautiful shoes in this sliver of a shop is made in Italy. The extensive selection includes lace-ups, slip-ons, sandals, boots, and slippers. All of the classic styles are always kept in stock, and, in addition, a limited selection of fine cashmere sweaters that any adult would covet—*golf* (cardigan) or *pullover*—are carried here.

Could it be purely accidental that just next door is a maternity shop that also sells baby clothes?

19

QUISQUILIA E PINZILLACCHERA

VIA PALAZZUOLO 13R

✉ ☎ 349 8301973 · *www.pezziunici.com*

MON 3:30-7PM; TUE-SAT 10AM-7PM

CLOSED SUNDAY

T HE UNWIELDY NAME FOR THIS MINISCULE SHOP IS A NOD TO A NONSENSICAL PHRASE BOR-rowed from the beloved Italian comedian Totò. Simona Catapano and Elena Targioni teamed up after studying at the Accademia di Belle Arti to create highly imaginative hats, puppets, dolls, and soft toys from boiled wool, felt, and cotton. All are handmade, and no two pieces are alike. The hats, which are whimsical works of sculpture, are wearable as well as highly decorative, and come in sizes and styles for men, women, and children. Bring a photo for a custom *bambola ritratto* (portrait doll).

[59]

OFFICINA PROFUMO FARMACEUTICA DI SANTA MARIA NOVELLA

20

VIA DELLA SCALA 16

▭ ☎ 055 216276 · *www.smnovella.it*

MON-SAT 9:30AM-7:30PM; SUN 10:30AM-7:30PM

YOU MAY HAVE SEEN THESE EXQUISITELY PACK-AGED SOAPS, LOTIONS, AND POTIONS IN OTHER locales, but a trip to the source is an experience not to be missed. Enter this cool, dark, seventeenth-century temple of *profumi* and you will find yourself transported to a sensuous other dimension.

A short distance from the church and piazza of the same name, Officina Profumo Farmaceutica di Santa Maria Novella is one of the world's oldest pharmacies. The Dominican fathers, who first arrived in Florence in 1221, collected herbs from the courtyard garden to create their own medicines for the monastery's infirmary, and then opened to the public in 1612.

A white-jacketed tribunal of sales clerks will assist you with the endless and enticing inventory of the Officina's essences and perfumes, which are still prepared according to the original formulas developed in 1500 for Caterina de' Medici. *Aceto dei Sette Ladri* (Vinegar of the Seven Thieves), whose recipe dates back to 1600, is still a favorite antidote for fainting spells. *Acqua Antisterica*, today sold as *Acqua di Santa Maria Novella*, for "a sedative and antispasmodic effect," was created by Fra'Angiolo Marchissi in 1614. The *Acqua di Rose*, a tonic to soothe red eyes, and the *Pasta di Mandorle*, a fragrant almond hand cream, are as beautiful as they are effective.

In recent years, the Officina di Santa Maria Novella revived the Dominican friars' ancient herbal remedy formulas for contemporary needs.

[63]

21

DOLCEFORTE

VIA DELLA SCALA 21R

☎ 055 219116

MON-SAT 10AM-1PM & 3:30-7:45PM; CLOSED SUNDAY

AFTER A TRIP TO THE HOLY SANCTUARY OF *PROFUMI* AT SANTA MARIA NOVELLA, INDULGE your senses further at Dolceforte. In winter, this sweet shop features only chocolate (primarily from Tuscany); many are trompe l'oeil, like their *atrezzi* (made to resemble tools, and dusted with cinnamon "rust"), or perfect replicas of salami and provolone. Purists will delight in Tuscan favorites such as Amedei (from an area outside of Pisa, dubbed the "Valley of Chocolate").

After Easter, when the temperature is less favorable for chocolate, marzipan makes an appearance, as do selected artisanal pastas, balsamic vinegar, *biscotti*, and delicious Sicilian jams and pestos.

[66]

BRONZISTA BALDINI

22

VIA PALAZZUOLO 101/103R

▭ ☎ 055 210933

MON-FRI 9AM-1PM & 3-7PM

CLOSED SATURDAY & SUNDAY

EVER SINCE IT WAS FOUNDED IN 1920 BY UBALDO BALDINI, FATHER OF THE CURRENT OWNER, THIS shop has been the destination for traditional bronze work, much of it made from original sixteenth-century models. In Baldini's hands, an encyclopedic collection of designs featuring angels, swans, cherubs, dolphins, lyres, flowers, and stars are crafted into door handles, cabinet pulls, sconces, towel racks, finials, keys, and keyhole plates. The pomegranate doorknob is a show-stopper. All work is made to order, in the back of the store, and takes about two months. Baldini's original shop sign still hangs proudly above the entrance.

CAPOCACCIA

(F) *Lungarno Corsini 12/14r* ▭ ☎ 055 210751
Lunch, dinner, aperitivi daily, closed Monday · Moderate

A place to see and be seen, this elegant frescoed salon, with doors
that open onto the Arno, serves delicious, eloquently-named panini,
along with salads and champagne by the glass. The beautiful young
Florentines keep Capocaccia hopping from *aperitivo* until late at
night, though one can enjoy a quiet lunch here as well.

CAFFÈ AMERINI

(G) *Via della Vigna Nuova 63r* ▭ ☎ 055 284941
Breakfast, lunch, aperitivi daily until 9:30pm · Moderate

Don't even *think* of asking for a menu. *"Il menù è la vetrina,"* greets
your host. In other words, choose from the glass case, place your order with the chic black-shirted young man behind the counter, find
a seat, eat, pay. Amerini is known for its fast service, fresh *insalatone*
(big salads) and panini, but especially for the glamorous clientele,
many of whom are impeccably-dressed shop clerks from nearby Via
de' Tornabuoni, eating lunch with their sunglasses on. You'll want
to stay all day for the nonstop parade of suits and furs.

MARIONE

Via della Spada 27r ▭ ☎ 055 214756 (H)

Lunch & dinner, closed Sunday · Inexpensive/Moderate

Hanging prosciuttos and salami greet you upon entering this warm, lively restaurant where locals come for good homemade pastas and *ribollita.* Lunch service is cordial albeit rushed; arrive early.

OSTERIA BELLE DONNE

Via delle Belle Donne 16r ▭ ☎ 055 2382609 (I)

Lunch & dinner daily · Moderate

Step into this restaurant-cum-Arcimbaldo-painting, with its fruit- and vegetable-festooned counter, for a seasonal menu served on colorful plates in a buzzing environment. Perch on stools while you literally rub elbows with noblemen, workers, and the occasional tourist. Inventive salads, fresh pastas and risottos, and daily soups make this a pleasant lunch or dinner destination.

AMON

Via Palazzuolo 28r ☎ 055 293146 (J)

Lunch & dinner, closed Monday · Inexpensive

Excellent falafel, couscous, kebabs, hummus, and tabouli, served with fresh-from-the-oven whole-wheat pita bread. Limited seating.

SHOPS

(23) Alinari

(24) Alice's Masks
Art Studio

(25) Fonte dei Dolci

(26) Mondo Albion

(27) Ida del Castillo Tessuti

(28) Falsi Gioielli

(29) BIVA

FOOD & DRINK

(K) Lobs

(L) Pepò

(M) Trattoria Antellesi

(N) Casa del Vino

ALINARI

LARGO ALINARI 15

▭ ☎ 055 23951 · *www.alinari.com*

MON 2:30-6:30PM; TUE-FRI 9AM-1PM & 2:30-6:30PM

SAT 9AM-1PM & 3-7PM; CLOSED SUNDAY

FOUNDED IN 1852, FRATELLI ALINARI IS THE OLD-EST PHOTOGRAPHY ARCHIVE IN THE WORLD. Housed along with the collection, the shop carries books, exhibition catalogues, and postcards, as well as matted and framed prints, all culled from the massive archive of beautiful black-and-white images. Prints (in either black-and-white or sepia) can be custom-ordered from the original glass-plate negatives.

Note: Alinari is easy to miss. Largo Alinari is at the intersection of Via Nazionale and Via Fiume, one block from the Piazza della Stazione. Look for number 15. If you are very tall or alert, you may spot a sign above the building entrance. Walk straight back to the courtyard, and look for the shop on the right.

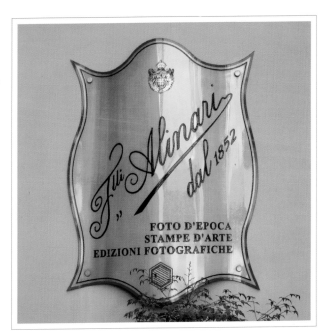

24

ALICE'S MASKS ART STUDIO

VIA FAENZA 72R

▭ ☎ 055 287370 · *www.alicemasks.com*

MON-SAT 9AM-1PM & 3:30-7:30PM; CLOSED SUNDAY

N O, YOU HAVEN'T JUST BEEN AIRLIFTED INTO VENETIAN CARNEVALE. THE SARDINIAN-BORN Agostino Dessi has been designing and producing papier-mâché masks in his Florence studio for over three decades. This shop hosts an ever-changing parade of devils and angels, suns and moons, rabbits, cats, birds, camels, harlequins, and Pinocchios; a face to suit your every mood. In 1997, Professor Dessi was joined by his daughter Alice, who works alongside her father at the back of the shop, and conducts a mask-making work-shop the last week of every month.

The duo's internationally-known masks are used for theater, film, and, of course, Carnevale in Venice.

[75]

A FLORENTINE WEDDING, CHRISTENING, FIRST COMMUNION, OR ANNIVERSARY WOULD BE unthinkable without *bomboniere* (a sort of elaborate party favor) from Fonte dei Dolci. An institution since 1954, the "Fountain of Sweets," a bright and inviting shop, takes great pride in its artful presentations of flowers and ribbon, using the finest candies. (A baptism, for instance, is heralded by a blue hot-air balloon with meticulously wrapped *confetti* piled inside the basket.)

But *bomboniere* comprise just a small part of this business. Fonte dei Dolci carries everything for the Tuscan sweet tooth: chocolates, hard candies, *palline di gomma* (colorful gum balls), *torrone*, *biscotti*, *panforte*, and *cassata fiorenza*, many of which are created in their own kitchens.

In addition to confections, Tuscan savories abound: pestos, crostini, porcini mushrooms, aged balsamic vinegars, extra-virgin olive oils, and pastas. (Look for the beautiful rose-colored *pasta al vino Chianti.*)

The enthusiastic sales staff generously offers samples, and will ship your order anywhere in the world.

MONDO ALBION

VIA NAZIONALE 121R

✎ ☎ 055 282451 · *www.mondoalbion.it*

MON-SAT 10AM-1PM; 3:30-7PM; CLOSED SUNDAY

IN A CITY OVERRUN WITH SHOE STORES, MONDO ALBION IS CERTAINLY THE MOST UNUSUAL. WITH his long white beard and eclectic wardrobe, Signor Albion designs handmade shoes that defy description. While his *calzaiolo* works at his craft at the front of the shop, Albion holds court amidst hundreds of unique pairs of colorful sandals, pumps, platforms, and boots— some perfect as Halloween attire, others quite wearable and comfortable. Still others are emblazoned with his distinctive prose, which also happens to appear on whatever he is wearing that day. No matter what your experience, you are likely to leave the shop with a unique pair of shoes and an unforgettable tale to go with them.

[81]

[82]

IDA DEL CASTILLO TESSUTI (27)

VIA XXVII APRILE 57/59R

▬ ☎ 055 481913

MON 3:30-7:30PM; TUE-SAT 9:30AM-7:30PM

CLOSED SUNDAY

IN A SERENE, AIRY SPACE NEAR THE PIAZZA DELLA INDIPENDENZA, IDA DEL CASTILLO WORKS with vividly-hued shimmering Thai silks and lush velvets to create an exquisite line of clothing and accessories for women. These unique designs for dresses, skirts, blouses, pants, scarves, shawls, handbags, brooches, and shoes are all made locally by hand, and are beautifully displayed in colorful rooms looking out onto a quiet courtyard. Lovely velvet-hemmed silk swing skirts, silk wrap blouses, and cashmere and velvet scarves and evening bags can be artfully gift-wrapped in two-tone mulberry paper by the very pleasant staff.

28

FALSI GIOIELLI

VIA DE' GINORI 34R

▭ ☎ 055 287237

MON 2:30-7:30PM; TUE-SAT 10AM-7:30PM

CLOSED SUNDAY

FOR 20 YEARS, SILVIA FRANCIOSI HAS BEEN ADORNING FLORENTINES IN *FALSI GIOIELLI* (fake jewelry)—bracelets, necklaces, earrings, hairpins, and barrettes—in a riotous spectrum of colors. Created from unusual vintage buttons, crystal, and Plexiglas, they are extremely whimsical and distinctive. While no one will ever mistake this jewelry for precious stones, it is attention-getting nonetheless, and for anywhere between one and 60 euros you can have your own conversation stopper. Whenever you choose to visit, you will find the staff quietly stringing beads at the back of the shop. Falsi Gioielli has another location, at Via dei Tavolini 5r.

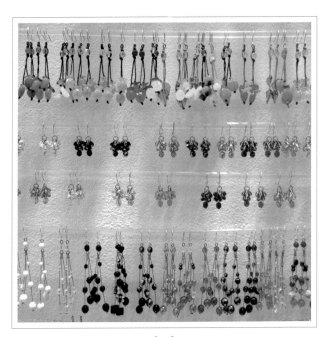

[85]

[86]

BIVA

29

VIA DELL'ARIENTO 8/10R

💳 ☎ 055 214391

9AM-7:30PM DAILY

MAKE THE EFFORT TO WEAVE YOUR WAY THROUGH THE CONGESTION OF STANDS IN the souk-like Mercato di San Lorenzo (watch for pickpockets) to the comparatively serene BIVA, home to every scarf your neck could ever desire. Silk, wool, cashmere, shantung, chiffon, and organza are here in patterns, solids, pleats, paisley—embroidered, fur-trimmed, even with pockets—in every color imaginable.

The seemingly endless inventory, all made in Italy, ranges in price from five to 65 euros, and also features matching shawls, ponchos, and handbags, as well as lovely umbrellas lined with contrasting fabrics, with wooden or jeweled handles. The helpful staff speaks English.

LOBS

Ⓚ *Via Faenza 75r* ▭ ☎ 055 212478
Lunch & dinner daily · Moderate

Fresh fish, deliciously and simply prepared, is a welcome departure from typical Florentine fare, as is the funky yet engaging maritime decor at Lobs (as in lobster). Warm rolls delivered to the table in a brown paper bag add to the charm. Good pastas are served at lunch.

PEPÒ

Ⓛ *Via Rosina 4/6r* ▭ ☎ 055 283259 · *www.pepo.it*
Lunch & dinner daily · Inexpensive/Moderate

Pepò is a breath of fresh air in an area once known for uninspired restaurants. Their simple, inexpensive lunch, served by a cheerful staff amidst a decor that is both modern and rustic, has made it a favorite among locals. The daily-changing menu features excellent pastas, soups, and main courses, using the freshest ingredients from the nearby Mercato Centrale. Try the *papardelle* with wild boar, or the *polpettine* (little meat balls).

TRATTORIA ANTELLESI
Via Faenza 9r ⬛ ☎ 055 216990
Lunch & dinner daily · Moderate

This warm and friendly restaurant serves hearty Tuscan home cooking on colorful hand-painted plates in a very pleasant setting. Antellesi features good homemade pastas and main courses that change seasonally, according to what is available at the market.

CASA DEL VINO
Via dell'Ariento 16r ⇌ ☎ 055 215609
www.casadelvino.it
Mon-Fri 9:30am-3:30pm, 5:30-8pm; Sat 10am-3:30pm
Closed Sunday · Inexpensive

An intimate space with dark carved wooden cabinetry and marble floors, Bruno and Gianni Migliorini's classic wine bar is a lively oasis in the frenetic San Lorenzo market. For a quick lunch or *aperitivo*, stand up at the bar and choose from a dozen reds or whites, or have the house Prosecco. Order from their massive selection of delicious €3 panini and crostini, and they will recommend a wine to pair with it.

Via San Zenobi
Via San Gallo
Via XXVII Aprile
Via Santa Reparata
Via Cavour
Via G. La Pira
Giardino dei Semplici
Via G. Capponi

(S)

(37)
(R)
Piazza San Marco

(38)

Via Guelfa

(36)

Via C. Battisti

SS. Annunziata

Galleria dell' Accademia

(39)

Via Taddea

Piazza del Mercato Centrale

Via delle Stufe

Via Cavour

Via degli Alfani

Piazza della SS. Annunziata

Museo Archeologico

Via della Colonna

Via Laura

(O)

(Q)

Via de' Ginori

Palazzo Medici Riccardi

Via Ricasoli

(34)

Via dei Servi

Via del Castellaccio

(35)

B S. Lorenzo

Via Martelli

Via de' Gori

Via de' Pucci

(32)

(P)

Via degli Alfani

(30)

(33)

Via M. Bufalini

Via della Pergola

Piazza San Giovanni

Duomo

(31)

[90]

SHOPS

(30) Scriptorium

(31) Gino Campani Cornici

(32) Alba

(33) Bartolini

(34) Oromatto

(35) Farmacia SS. Annunziata

(36) Libreria Lef

(37) Pugi

(38) Maison Rouge

(39) Libreria del Cinema

FOOD & DRINK

(O) Carabe

(P) Caffellatte

(Q) Robiglio

(R) Pugi

(S) Ristorante da Mimmo

SCRIPTORIUM

VIA DEI SERVI 5R

☎ 055 211804 · *www.scriptoriumfirenze.com*

MON-SAT 10AM-2PM & 3:30-7:30PM

CLOSED SUNDAY

A PASSION FOR THE ART OF WRITING IS IMME-DIATELY APPARENT IN THIS CHARMING SHOP. Not far from the convent of San Marco, where Dominican monks toiled at their illuminated manuscripts, this ancient craft is still alive and well at Scriptorium, which sells everything for the lover of handmade books and calligraphy. From their own signature inks, pens, and blank books, to fine leather-covered boxes, to personalized stationery stamped in gold, Scriptorium has everything for the modern-day scribe.

If your purchase is a gift, the helpful staff will gladly wrap it for you with *carta paglia*, twine, and sealing wax.

31

GINO CAMPANI CORNICI

VIA DEI SERVI 22R

☎ 055 216984

MON–SAT 9AM–12:30PM & 3:30–7:30PM

CLOSED SUNDAY

JUST STEPS FROM THE DUOMO, IN THE TINY PIAZZETTA OF THE CHURCH OF S. MICHELE VISdomini, the skilled artisans of Gino Campani Cornici have been practicing their craft since 1889. Quality handmade frames of every type of wood, in every style —gilded, carved, stained, inlaid—are available readymade or to order. (The custom frames are made in the back of the shop and take about a week to complete.)

A selection of botanical prints, hand-colored engravings, maps, and classic scenes of Florence and Tuscany is also available for purchase.

[96]

ALBA

VIA DEI SERVI 25/27/29R

▭ ☎ 055 287754 · *www.abbigliamento-lavoro.it*

MON-FRI 9AM-1PM & 3:30-7:30PM; SAT 9AM-1PM

CLOSED SUNDAY

THIS UNIFORM STORE HAS BEEN DRESSING FLOR-ENTINE PROFESSIONALS STYLISHLY SINCE 1956. Together with neighbor Bartolini (see page 98), Alba can help you look and cook just like a bonafide Italian chef, outfitting you in toques (cloth or paper), neckerchiefs, jackets, pants (checked or striped), and clogs. Or consider their classic waiter's and maid's uniforms, aprons, and vests. The shop also features rubber gloves in a range of fluorescent colors, and sensible shoes to go with every outfit. All styles are available either ready to wear, or made to order, and can be personalized with hand embroidery.

BARTOLINI

VIA DEI SERVI 30R

☎ 055 211895 · *www.dinobartolini.it*

MON 3:30-7:30PM; TUE-SAT 10AM-1PM & 3:30-7:30PM

CLOSED SUNDAY

IF A KITCHEN GADGET EXISTS, EXPECT TO FIND IT AT BARTOLINI. FOR OVER SEVENTY YEARS, THIS store has been the source for all things for the professional and home cook: pots and pans, knives, espresso machines, crystal (more than 200 styles of wine and drinking glasses), and cutlery (well over 130 services, from the most elegant to everyday). Room after room offers a dizzying array of wares for every taste and budget. If you happen to be interested in a pasta machine, you can choose from the popular Imperia brand found in most Italian homes, or the more artisanal *chitarra* (resembling a guitar) for hand-cut pasta.

34

OROMATTO

VIA DEI SERVI 49R

▭ ☎ 055 216768

MON-SAT 10AM-1PM & 4-7:30PM

CLOSED SUNDAY

IF YOU'VE HAD YOUR FILL OF THE RENAISSANCE, ANNA GAZZI'S LIVELY COLLECTION OF VINTAGE costume jewelry offers a refreshing change of pace.

In this shop no bigger than a bijoux box, bracelets, brooches, necklaces, and earrings crafted in Bakelite, Lucite, rhinestones, and jet are culled from the 1950s to the 1980s. The *oromatto* ("fake gold") is lovingly selected, and is arranged thematically for the ever-changing window displays. Gazzi's personal preference for black and white is evident in some spectacular specimens, all of which are reasonably priced.

[101]

FARMACIA SS. ANNUNZIATA ㉟

VIA DEI SERVI 80R

☎ 055 210738 · *www.ker.it*

MON-SAT 9AM-1PM & 4-8PM

CLOSED SUNDAY

IN 1561, HERBALIST AND CHEMIST DOMENICO DI VINCENZO BRUNETTI MOVED HIS SHOP TO A charming vaulted space on Via dei Servi. Today, the same sculpted dark wood cabinets of the Farmacia SS. Annunziata are still stocked with their exclusive line of natural products in simple yet elegant signature black-and-white packaging, all handmade using the original formulas. Choose from a delectable menu of skin- and hair-care products for men, women, and children: rosemary and sage soap, calendula exfoliating cream, almond bath gel, sage toothpaste, ginkgo hair conditioner, carrot suntan oil, bilberry aftershave, and chamomile baby shampoo.

36

LIBRERIA LEF

VIA RICASOLI 105/107R

▭ ☎ 055 216533 · *www.librerialef.it*

MON-FRI 9AM-7:30PM

SAT 9AM-1:30PM & 3:30-7:30PM; CLOSED SUNDAY

IF THE WAIT TO VIEW MICHELANGELO'S *DAVID* BECOMES UNBEARABLE, HAVE SOMEONE HOLD your place on line and run directly across the street to the conveniently-located Libreria Lef.

Specialists in books on architecture, design (interior, industrial, and graphic), photography, urban planning, and fine arts, they also carry a selection of European DVDs, postcards, maps, and prints. The softspoken, efficient staff will be happy to assist you.

And should you become too comfortable and decide to forego the queue across the street, Lef also has books on the Accademia's most famous resident.

[104]

[105]

37

PUGI

PIAZZA SAN MARCO 10

✆ 055 280981 · *www.focacceria-pugi.it*

MON-SAT 7:45AM-8PM

CLOSED SUNDAY

THE EVER-CONSTANT THRONG OF FLORENTINES WAITING FOR THEIR BELOVED FOCACCIA TO emerge from the oven is a testament to Pugi's genius. A local institution, this bakery creates sublime pizza, focaccia, and *schiacciata* in every imaginable combination: plain, stuffed or topped with vegetables, and in autumn, with wine grapes, sugar, and fennel seed. You can eat standing up, or they will wrap it for you (but who can wait?). They also carry delicious *torte di frutta*, *biscotti di Prato*, and *frittelle di riso* (sweet rice fritters).

Pugi is conveniently located in front of the Piazza San Marco bus stop, and, happily, has no midday closing.

[108]

MAISON ROUGE

VIA CAVOUR 82R

☎ 055 280342

MON-SAT 10AM-7PM

CLOSED SUNDAY

MAISON ROUGE'S SIGNATURE BLOUSES, DRESSES, SWEATERS, SKIRTS, AND JACKETS ARE LUSH, romantic fashions evocative of another era; irresistible, ornate combinations of lace, linen, chenille, and velvet, in Victorian styles that are ultra-feminine yet exceedingly comfortable.

In winter, confections of lace and velvet delight and flatter; in spring and summer, dresses of delicate embroidered pastel linen with lace make their appearance. All are handmade locally.

Maison Rouge has two other small shops in the Centro Storico: Via dello Studio 9r, and Piazza del Duomo 51r.

LIBRERIA DEL CINEMA

VIA GUELFA 14R

☎ 055 216416

TUE-SAT 10AM-2PM & 3:30-7PM

CLOSED SUNDAY & MONDAY

As A FILM STUDENT FRUSTRATED BY A LACK OF BOOKSTORES DEVOTED TO CINEMA, TOMASSO Feraci had no choice but to open his own shop. Nine years later, the Libreria del Cinema is still the only one of its kind in Florence, carrying books, posters, calendars, movie stills, and postcards. A selection of Italian and foreign films on DVD and video include some of Feraci's personal favorites: Fellini, Rossellini, Truffaut, and Bergman. (Note that European DVDs and videos are not operable on American machines, although both Mac and Windows DVD drives will play non-US discs if you change the region code preference on your computer.)

CARABE

(O) *Via Ricasoli 60r* ✏ ☎ 055 289476
Daily 9am-1am · Inexpensive

The Sicilian owners, emphatic about using only seasonal ingredients, make superb fruit- and nut-flavored gelato. For a breakfast you'll never forget, order their coffee granita with whipped cream and a brioche. You won't see cannoli on display, as they are made to order, but are well worth asking for.

CAFFELLATTE

(P) *Via degli Alfani 39r* ✏ ☎ 055 2478878
Mon-Sat 8am-8pm; Sun 10am-7pm · Moderate

Located in a former dairy (the sign still reads *Latteria*), Caffellatte serves organically grown vegetarian fare all day long. Organic coffees and teas, homemade soups, salads, pastas, and freshly baked scones are offered in a comfortable and politically correct setting.

ROBIGLIO

(Q) *Via dei Servi 112r* ▭ ☎ 055 212784
Mon-Sat 8am-8pm, closed Sunday & August · Moderate

Have a light lunch of a salad or panini, or savor a cappuccino or *torta* at this classic Florentine pasticceria. Robiglio has another location in the Centro, but this one is by far the better of the two.

PUGI

Piazza San Marco 10 🚫 ☎ 055 280981
www.focacceria-pugi.it
Mon-Sat 7:45am-8pm · Inexpensive
(see shop 37, p. 106)

RISTORANTE DA MIMMO

Via San Gallo 57/59r 🍽 ☎ 055 481030 Ⓢ
Mon-Sat Lunch & dinner, Sat and Sun Dinner only · Moderate
Housed in a former theater, with a dramatic seventeenth-century frescoed ceiling, Ristorante da Mimmo sports voluptuous garlands of fresh vegetables hanging over the entry to the bar area, and is well-loved by locals for excellent cuisine and quick, cheerful service. At lunch, the ever-changing *Menu del Lavoratore* (Worker's Menu) offers a choice of pastas, *insalatone*, and main courses at very reasonable prices. Order the *porchetta* (stuffed and rolled baby pork), and Mimmo himself will slice it for you at your table.

At dinner, the white tablecloths come out and the prices go up, but it is a delicious and memorable dining experience nonetheless.

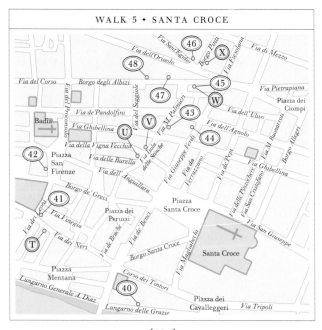

SHOPS

(40) Del Moro

(41) Jamie Marie Lazzara

(42) Al Portico

(43) Libreria Salimbeni

(44) Filistrucchi

(45) Vestri

(46) Sbigoli Terrecotte

(47) Cartoleria Ecologica
La Tartaruga

(48) Elisir

FOOD & DRINK

(T) All'Antico Vinaio

(U) Vivoli

(V) Osteria Caffè Italiano

(W) Vestri

(X) La Giostra

DEL MORO

LUNGARNO DELLE GRAZIE 18

▭ ☎ 055 2346523

MON-SAT 10AM-7PM; CLOSED SUNDAY

GIVEN THIS SHOP'S ROMANTIC VIEW OF THE ARNO, IT'S NOT DIFFICULT TO IMAGINE DEL Moro's original customers strolling through the streets of Florence in their chic cloches or floppy wide-brims festooned with feathers or flowers. Since 1931, this family-run *cappelleria* has been outfitting women in exquisite headwear. Now under the direction of the founder's granddaughter Sara, Del Moro uses the finest velvet, merino wool, leather, felt, and straw to produce original handmade hats for all occasions using traditional wooden molds. These creations are made on the premises, and many are used for theatrical productions, where the shop's historical expertise is invaluable.

[117]

41

JAMIE MARIE LAZZARA

VIA DEI LEONI 4R

✆ 055 280573

MON-FRI 9:30AM-1PM & 3:30-7PM;

SATURDAY BY APPOINTMENT; CLOSED SUNDAY

ONE IS RELUCTANT TO DISTURB JAMIE MARIE LAZZARA AS SHE PAINSTAKINGLY WORKS IN the silence of her tiny shop filled with violin parts. A prodigy at the age of eight, she came to Italy nearly three decades ago to study violinmaking. Now a *Maestro Liutaio*, as her classic gold-leaf sign proclaims, Lazzara creates and repairs violins and violas for many celebrated musicians. She is especially proud to have crafted Itzhak Perlman's first modern instrument. Director Ridley Scott was so taken with the shop that it inspired a scene in his 2001 film *Hannibal*, which was shot in Florence.

[119]

[120]

AL PORTICO

PIAZZA SAN FIRENZE 1

☎ 055 21316 · *www.semialportico.it*

MON-FRI 8:30AM-7:30PM; SUN 10AM-5PM

HOUSED IN THE COURTYARD OF THE STATELY PALAZZO GONDI (BUILT IN 1492 AND STILL IN-habited by the family), Al Portico is a soothing refuge from the chaos of neighborhood leather boutiques. Circling a central stone fountain is everything for the gardening enthusiast: beautiful flowering plants (including gardenias year-round), terra cotta pots, even *Pezzi di David* (facsimile fragments of Michelangelo's famous statue). Seductively packaged seeds of every variety are hard to pass up, green thumb notwithstanding.

If you choose to purchase cut flowers as a gift, owner Maurizia Venturi will be happy to advise you on the best way to make a *bella figura*.

LIBRERIA SALIMBENI

VIA M. PALMIERI 14/16R

☎ 055 2340904 · *www.libreriasalimbeni.com*

MON-SAT 10AM-1PM & 4-7:30PM; CLOSED SUNDAY

FROM ITS MODEST BEGINNINGS IN 1940 AS A SCRAP PAPER STORE, LIBRERIA SALIMBENI IS today one of the most highly regarded bookstores for art and antiquarian subjects. Nineteen sixty-six saw the launch of Salimbeni's own publishing company, and although the first book suffered an untimely debut just days before the flood, the imprint continued through the 1990s to publish notable facsimile editions of Futurist books and periodicals, many of which are still available.

Presently, the second generation of Salimbeni, siblings Serenella and Stefano, continue the family tradition in offering an impressive catalogue (also available online) and expert service.

44

FILISTRUCCHI

VIA G. VERDI 9

☎ 055 2344901 · *www.filistrucchi.it*

MON 3-7PM; TUE-FRI 8:30AM-12:30PM

& 3-7PM; SAT 3-7PM; CLOSED SUNDAY

FILISTRUCCHI IS A LEADING EXPERT IN THE PRO-
DUCTION OF HUMAN-HAIR WIGS AND BEARDS,
papier-mâché masks, makeup, and special effects for
film, theater, and television. The business has flourished
in the same location, under the direction of the same
family, since 1720. Although it has survived two major
floods (in 1844 and 1966), the interior has remained vir-
tually intact. All work is done on the premises, in the
upstairs laboratory.

While both father and son respectfully decline to
name names, it is clear that their clientele includes in-
ternationally renowned actors and actresses.

[125]

[126]

VESTRI

BORGO DEGLI ALBIZI 11R

☎ 055 2340374 · *www.vestri.it*

MON-SAT 10:30AM-8PM; CLOSED SUNDAY & AUGUST

ADVICE TO A CHOCOHOLIC VISITING FLORENCE: CHOOSE A HOTEL AS CLOSE AS POSSIBLE TO Vestri, on the Borgo degli Albizi.

Made in Arezzo laboratories in copper pots, these intense, artisanal chocolates flavored with chili pepper, nuts, apricots, oranges, or espresso, are truly addictive. Florentines look forward to warmer weather, when Vestri's creamy, dreamy, chocolate gelato spiked with mint, cayenne, hazelnut, and other enticing flavors is hand-scooped by Leonardo Vestri himself.

For the ultimate indulgence, try a shot of sumptuous *cioccolata da bere* (drinkable chocolate)—hot in winter, cold in summer, and always delicious.

SBIGOLI TERRECOTTE

VIA SANT'EGIDIO 4R

☎ 055 2479713 · *www.sbigoliterrecotte.it*

MON-SAT 9AM-1PM & 3-7:30PM; CLOSED SUNDAY

ORIGINALLY FOUNDED IN 1857, AND A FAMILY OPERATION SINCE 1966, SBIGOLI FEATURES beautiful Tuscan hand-painted terra cotta in traditional as well as contemporary designs. The shop is a colorful extravaganza of gaily-decorated plates, urns, pitchers, serving pieces, tea and espresso sets, custom signs, house numbers, lamps, sundials, terra-cotta-topped tables on wrought iron bases, glazed earthenware cooking pots, and unglazed pots for the garden or terrace.

Antonella Adami, born into a family of ceramicists, and her daughter Lorenza, at work at the back of the shop, will help you select and ship home the perfect piece of pottery.

[129]

47

CARTOLERIA ECOLOGICA LA TARTARUGA

BORGO DEGLI ALBIZI 60R

▭ ☎ 055 2340845

MON-SAT 9:30AM-7:30PM; CLOSED SUNDAY

FOR NEARLY 25 YEARS, IRANIAN-BORN VIDA MOKHTARI HAS BEEN DELIGHTING FLORENTINES of all ages with her selection of ecological toys and objects. The store is chock-a-block with wonderful wrapping papers, wooden toys, unusual journals, and blank books, all made by local artisans from eco-friendly materials. Choose from charming *quaderni* (traditional notebooks for schoolchildren) in the classic style of the 1940s, wooden puppets, jumping jacks, puzzles, kaleidoscopes, mobiles, or tiny hand-painted wooden clothespins with (or without) a ladybug attached. Nothing plastic or fluorescent is allowed in the store's inventory.

48

ELISIR

BORGO DEGLI ALBIZI 70R

▭ ☎ 055 2638218

MON 3:30-7:30PM; TUE-SAT 10AM-7:30PM

CLOSED SUNDAY

ONCE INSIDE THIS AIRY INTERIOR WITH ITS MAGNIFICENT FRESCOED CEILING, YOU WILL be seduced further by the subtle scents and exquisite packaging of this lovely shop's selection of European natural fragrances and cosmetics. Wander through two heavenly-perfumed rooms filled with the likes of Floris, Penhaligon, Diptych, Lorenzo Villoresi, L'Artisan, and Czech & Speake.

The helpful staff will be happy to guide you in finding your own personal fragrance.

[133]

ALL'ANTICO VINAIO

(T)

Via dei Neri 65r 🍴 ☎ 055 2382723

Tue-Sun 8am-8pm, closed Monday & August · Inexpensive

Neighborhood residents make a practice of gathering here after work for a glass of Daniele's recommended Chianti, and to sample his sumptuous array of antipasti. A lively and entertaining spot to eat, drink, and catch up on the events of the day.

VIVOLI

(U)

Via Isola delle Stinche 7r 🚫 ☎ 055 292334

Tue-Sun 8am-1am, closed Monday · Inexpensive

Vivoli is one of Florence's best-loved gelaterias. Follow the trail of discarded cups along Via Isola delle Stinche and try the dark chocolate with bitter orange, carmelized pear, or amaretto *semifreddo*.

OSTERIA CAFFÈ ITALIANO

(V)

Via Isola delle Stinche 11r 🍴 ☎ 055 289368

Lunch & dinner Tue-Sun, closed Monday · Moderate

With its vaulted ceiling, wrought-iron chandelier, and dark wood paneling, this is a perfect place to while away an afternoon over a *pappa al pomodoro* (tomato and bread soup) or *spaghetti alla carbonara*. While lunch is reasonably priced, dinner can be a bit steep. An excellent selection of wines is available by the glass.

VESTRI

Borgo degli Albizi 11r 📠 ☎ 055 2340374
www.vestri.it
Mon-Sat 10:30am-8pm, closed Sunday · Inexpensive
(see shop 45, p. 127)

LA GIOSTRA

Borgo Pinti 10r 📠 ☎ 055 241341
www.ristorantelagiostra.com
Lunch & dinner daily · Moderate

What a delight to be greeted by the elegant and charming chef/owner/prince (really) with a complimentary glass of Prosecco and assorted *crostini*. Try the thinly-sliced artichokes, or, in season, the *tagliarini* with white truffles. Once a storage space for the Piazza dei Ciompi's merry-go-round (*la giostra* in Italian), this restaurant is pure magic. The twinkling lights add to the festive atmosphere, as does the miniature treasure chest that your check will arrive in. Reservations are a must.

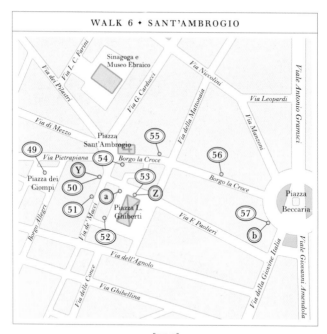

SHOPS

(49) Mercato delle Pulci

(50) Cibreo Teatro del Sale

(51) Sandra Dori

(52) Angela Salamone

(53) Mercato di Sant'Ambrogio

(54) Mesticheria Mazzanti

(55) L'Elefante Verde

(56) Antica Officina del Farmicista Dr. Vranjes

(57) Dolci & Dolcezze

FOOD & DRINK

(Y) Cibreo Teatro del Sale

(Z) Trattoria da Rocco

(a) Gilda

(b) Dolci & Dolcezze

MERCATO DELLE PULCI

PIAZZA DEI CIOMPI
≠ TUE-SAT 10AM-7PM
LAST SUNDAY OF THE MONTH (EXCEPT JULY)

THIS SLEEPY LITTLE FLEA MARKET COMPRISED OF 29 DEALERS IS OPEN DAILY (NO MIDDAY CLOSing) and is located in the Piazza dei Ciompi, named after the woolworkers of medieval Florence. Everything from genuine antiques to pure junk can be found here: vintage tins, buttons, photographs, jewelry, books, postcards, lace, perfume bottles, light fixtures, and tools. It is hard to leave without at least one new find, and, if nothing else, the relaxed attitude of the dealers can be refreshing.

On the last Sunday of the month (except July), the market spills into the entire piazza, with nearly 100 dealers, affording more exciting prospects.

[139]

(50) CIBREO TEATRO DEL SALE

VIA DE' MACCI 111R

☎ 055 2001492 · *www.teatrodelsale.com*

TUE-SAT BREAKFAST, LUNCH, AND DINNER

CLOSED SUNDAY, MONDAY & AUGUST

IN A CITY OF SO MANY OPINIONS, PARTICULARLY WHEN IT COMES TO FOOD, EVERYONE SEEMS TO be in agreement that Fabbio Picchi of Cibreo is the best chef/restaurateur. His transformation of a tiny neighborhood near the Mercato di Sant'Ambrogio has become nothing less than an empire of Florentine cuisine. Picchi begs to differ: *"Non è un impero—è una città!"* (It's not an empire—it's a city!) The most recent addition to his already legendary restaurant, trattoria, and *caffè* is Cibreo Teatro del Sale—a private club housed in a cavernous fourteenth-century former convent. For a mere five euros, one can become a *socio* (member),

signing a contract to abide by the rules. Membership privileges include breakfast, lunch, and dinner at very reasonable prices. Dinner consists of a live performance, in addition to Picchi's in the kitchen, neither of which should be missed.

The shop, which greets you at the entrance to the theater, and is open to members and non-members alike, sells a variety of carefully selected products, from Cibreo's own preserved vegetables and *marmellate*, to patés, carnaroli rice, honey from the isle of Elba, bath products by Lorenzo Villoresi, and local wines. Look for Cibreo's signature *bicchieri riciclati* (recycled drinking glasses). Cut down from wine bottles and used in the restaurant, they are a bargain at four euros each (or spring for the gift box of eight for 30 euros).

Once you purchase your membership card, make a reservation for dinner, which starts promptly at 7:30 pm. Picchi, working in his massive glassed-in kitchen, prepares course after course and dramatically announces each as it is sent to the buffet table: *"Risotto del Principe!"* He will holler out suggestions as well: Don't eat too much bread; don't mix your salad with the rest of the food on your plate; pace yourself. Best of all, pasta dishes, which do not appear on the menu in his other restaurants, are here in full force. After an amazing meal, the kitchen blinds are drawn, chairs turn toward the stage, and the evening's entertainment begins—anything from a string quartet to standup comedy—arranged by Picchi's wife, Maria Cassi, who, as entertainment director, sometimes performs herself.

A visit to Florence is not complete without a trip to the *città* of Cibreo.

51

SANDRA DORI

VIA DE' MACCI 103R

✉ ☎ 348 3574726 · *arteoggetti103.com*

MON 3:30-7:30PM, TUE-SAT 9AM-1PM, 3:30-7:30PM

CLOSED SUNDAY

EN ROUTE TO THE MERCATO DI SANT'AMBROGIO, IT IS WELL WORTH A DETOUR TO SANDRA DORI'S delightful shop to see her unique interpretations of *paralumi* (lampshades). Fashioned from unusual materials such as mosaics and inlaid leathers, these are functional works of art. If you can't decide between the straw hat with flowers, or one inspired by a classic Sicilian donkey cart, she will design to order. Dori also creates lovely *nappe* (tassels) from shells, beads, and other unique materials, as well as pillows and wall hangings. Her simple yet beautiful handmade rose pins crafted from pastel shades of leather make a perfect and portable gift.

[145]

[146]

ANGELA SALAMONE

PIAZZA L. GHIBERTI 16R

 ☎ 055 2346811

MON 4-7PM; TUE-SAT 10AM-1PM, 4-7PM

CLOSED SUNDAY

THE NORWEGIAN-SICILIAN ANGELA SALAMONE BRINGS NEW LIFE TO THE ART OF TRADITIONAL bookbinding with her line of modernist albums, notebooks, frames, folders, and portfolios created from paper, cotton, and linen. In this tiny, light-filled corner shop opposite the Sant'Ambrogio market, the soft-spoken Salamone, who studied both art and philosophy in Florence, creates meticulously crafted pieces in brilliant hues of fuschia, tangerine, and lavender, using a combination of traditional Italian and Japanese techniques.

Allow time for gift wrapping, which in Salamone's hands is an art in itself.

MERCATO DI SANT'AMBROGIO

PIAZZA L. GHIBERTI

MON-SAT 8AM-1PM; CLOSED SUNDAY

THE SANT'AMBROGIO MARKET'S INTIMATE SCALE AND EXCELLENT PRODUCE MAKE IT A FAVORite among Florentines, who flock to the Piazza Ghiberti with their oversized shopping totes.

The bustling outdoor section features the freshest seasonal local fare—tantalizing displays of fruits, vegetables, cheeses, and *salumi*. As a contest ensues to see which vendor can outshout the other, one hears cries of *"Freschissimo!"* ("The freshest!") The edibles are juxtaposed with a cheerful hodgepodge of constantly changing wares: clothing, intimate apparel, shoes, baby clothes, table linens, household items, notions, and cut flowers—all at extremely reasonable prices.

[149]

Step inside the airy, hanger-like interior (where you will be greeted by a large mosaic Florentine lily on the floor) for a delicious choice of stands selling meats, pastas, oils, fresh fish, and coffees, as well as a *caffè* and trattoria (see page 162).

The *mercato* gets high marks for conveniences; clean bathrooms are available downstairs for 60 *centesimi*, and bike rentals can be arranged at the far end of the market (between the flower stalls and the parking garage) by the hour or by the day.

Mariangela Catalani, owner of the charming bed and breakfast Le Stanze di Santa Croce, gives guided tours of the market in conjunction with her cooking classes: *www.lestanzedisantacroce.com.*

[151]

54

MESTICHERIA MAZZANTI

BORGO LA CROCE 101R

✗ ☎ 055 2480663

MON-SAT 8AM-1PM & 3:30-7:30PM

CLOSED SUNDAY & AUGUST

THE TRANSLATION OF *MESTICHERIA* (HARDWARE STORE) DOES NOT DO JUSTICE TO THIS SHOP, a celebration of all things for the everyday household. Room after room is jam-packed with brightly colored dishcloths, festively patterned cheesecloth by the meter, wine glasses, espresso cups, and glazed terra cotta pots for oven or stovetop cooking. Disposable placemats made from *carta paglia* (a rough ochre-colored paper once used in butcher shops) are easy to roll up and take home. In summer, you'll find practical items such as innovative mosquito repellents and *coprifrutta a rete*, a three-tiered netted cage to protect fruit from unwanted visitors.

[153]

[154]

L'ELEFANTE VERDE

BORGO LA CROCE 70/72R

▭ ☎ 055 2342882

MON-SAT 10AM-1PM & 5-8PM

CLOSED SUNDAY

INSPIRED BY FREQUENT TRIPS TO THE FAR EAST, LORIANA BERGANTINI DESIGNS ELEGANT AND innovative skirts, blouses, jackets, coats, slippers, pillows, and curtains that fill her tiny shop on the Borgo La Croce. Exploding with color, all items are handmade by local artisans from shimmering Italian and Indian silks. If you don't find something in your size, it can be made to order and sent to you within a week to ten days.

The charming and stylish Bergantini, always dressed in one or more of her creations, serves as the best advertising for this lovely shop.

ANTICA OFFICINA DEL FARMICISTA DR. VRANJES

BORGO LA CROCE 44R

☎ 055 241748 · *www.drvranjes.it*

MON 3:30-7:30PM; TUE-SAT 10AM-1PM & 3:30-7:30PM

CLOSED SUNDAY

THIS EXQUISITELY SCENTED SHOP/*LABORATORIO*, AN AIRY SPACE STOCKED WITH SHIMMERING bottles, is where Dr. Paolo Vranjes, born and raised in Bologna, practices the art of aromatherapy. Elegant apothecary bottles are filled with handmade fragrances, crafted from fine essential oils and natural ingredients, for personal and home use. Vranjes interprets scents as varied as the Mediterranean, a Tuscan garden, and *Fiori di Sicilia*, for the home, body, and wardrobe.

The walls of this gleaming interior are adorned with botanical prints from Studio Puck (see page 184).

57

DOLCI & DOLCEZZE

PIAZZA BECCARIA 8R

≠ ☎ 055 2345458

TUE-SAT 8:30AM-8PM; SUN 9AM-1PM & 4:30-7:30PM

CLOSED MONDAY

ON THE LOVELY, LESS TOURIST-TRAVELED PIAZZA BECCARIA, DOLCI & DOLCEZZE IS AS arresting to the eye as it is to the palate. With its elegant mint-lacquered facade and strikingly beautiful interior of oil paintings, crystal chandeliers, and inlaid marble floor, this diminutive *pasticceria* presents its signature flourless chocolate cake and delicious fresh fruit tarts, along with a selection of equally intriguing savories.

Having no professional training and just a passion for inventive baking, Ilaria Ballatresi started the shop with her husband, Giulio, 27 years ago. Since his death, she has maintained the business with her two children,

exacting the same high standards: only the best-quality ingredients, in season, are used.

In winter, look for *marrons glacés* and chocolates, while in summer, magic is made with all seasonal fruits. Stand at the bar and enjoy a cappuccino or hot chocolate served in an elegant china cup while contemplating the shelves of beautifully displayed *marmellate*, *gianduja*, Caffè Piansa, and *biscotti*.

It would be difficult to leave Dolci & Dolcezze without taking note of the plaque that states, *"Sono la torta al cioccolata più buona del mondo."* (I am the world's best chocolate cake.) This is no exaggeration.

[161]

CIBREO TEATRO DEL SALE

(Y)

Via de' Macci 111r 🚻 ☎ 055 2001492
www.teatrodelsale.com
Breakfast, lunch, and dinner Tue-Sat
(Reservations are required for dinner)
Closed Sunday, Monday & August · Moderate
(see shop 50, p. 140)

TRATTORIA DA ROCCO

Inside the Mercato di Sant'Ambrogio

(Z)

Piazza L. Ghiberti 🚫 ☎ 339 8384555
Mon-Sat 12-3pm · Inexpensive

Fresh, good, cheap, and fast is what you will find at this no-frills lunch spot in the bustling market. *Primi piatti* such as *pappa al pomodoro* and lasagne *alla genovese* are priced at €2.50; *secondi* (*pollo arrosto, melanzana ripieno*) are only €3.

GILDA

Piazza L. Ghiberti 40/41r 🍴 ☎ 055 2343885

Breakfast, lunch, and dinner, closed Sunday · Moderate

This small, eclectic bistro's proximity to the Sant'Ambrogio market ensures fresh, seasonal dishes that are delicious and reasonably priced. Reservation notwithstanding, you may have to wait for a table, in which case the *simpaticissima* Gilda will set you up at the bar, where you can enjoy the lively local scene while savoring a dish of heavenly polenta with a baroque goblet of white wine.

DOLCI & DOLCEZZE

Piazza Beccaria 8r 🚫 ☎ 055 2345458

Tue-Sat 8:30am-8pm; Sun 9am-1pm, 4:30-7:30pm, closed Monday
Moderate (see shop 57, p. 158)

Standing room only, but who cares when you are experiencing the world's best chocolate cake?

Ponte Amerigo
Vespucci

Borgo Ognissanti

FIUME ARNO

Via della Vigna Nuova

Via del Parione

Lungarno Amerigo Vespucci

58

Via le Mura
di Santa Rosa

Via Sant'Onofrio

Via L. Bartolini

Lungarno Soderini

Piazza
di Cestello

Ponte alla
Carraia

Lungarno Corsini

59

Borgo San Frediano

61

62

e

64

Ponte Santa
Trinita

Viale F. Arnolfo

Via S. Cristoforo

60

Piazza
dei Nerli

Via del Drago d'Oro

Lungarno
Guicciardini

67

Via dell'Orto

c

Via Santo Spirito

Piazza del
Carmine

Borgo Stella

65

Via Cantarella

Via della Leone

Via
Santa Monaca

63

66

68

f

Via Canदन् maldoli

Santa Maria
del Carmine

d

Via dell'Ardiglione

Via Sant'Agostino

Via Malfia

Piazza
Santo
Spirito

Via de' Velluti

Piazza
Torquato
Tasso

Via della Chiesa

Via dei Serragli

Piazza
de'Pitti

Via Toscanella

Giardino
Torrigiani

Via del Campuccio

Via delle Caldaie

Via Mazzetta

Via di Presto
di San Martino

Via Maggio

Palazzo
Pitti

Via Francesco Petrarca

SHOPS

(58) Antico Setificio Fiorentino   (64) Francesco da Firenze

(59) Brandimarte   (65) Castorina

(60) Stefano Bemer   (66) Studio Puck

(61) Il Paralume   (67) Aprosio & Co

(62) Twisted   (68) Olio & Convivium

(63) Ceri Vintage

FOOD & DRINK

(c) Trattoria del Carmine   (e) Il Santo Bevitore

(d) Cavolo Nero   (f) Olio & Convivium

ANTICO SETIFICIO FIORENTINO

VIA L. BARTOLINI 4

☎ 055 213861 · *setificiofiorentino.it*

MON-FRI 9AM-1PM & 2-5PM (BY APPOINTMENT)

CLOSED SATURDAY & SUNDAY

ON VIA BARTOLINI, LOOK FOR A WROUGHT-IRON GATE AND A NUMBER FOUR WHICH IS NEITHER red nor black. (There is actually a sign for Antico Setificio Fiorentino, though it is partially obscured by climbing vines.) Ring the buzzer under number four, and walk straight ahead to another gate, where you will be buzzed in to another century.

An idyllic courtyard is silent except for the hypnotic sound of swallows, and the rhythmical hum of the original eighteenth-century looms from the adjacent *laboratorio*. Once inside the showroom, bolts of colorful

[167]

shimmering silks, brilliant damasks, and opulent brocades fill room after room. *Ermisino*, a particular type of taffeta, is woven exclusively here. The fabrics are the same that are depicted in the paintings of Masaccio, Bronzino, and Piero della Francesca.

While the Antico Setificio's list of clients can be intimidating (the Kremlin, the Royal Palaces of Stockholm, and the Quirinale in Rome), the curtains, bedspreads, silk and cashmere scarves, and silk bags filled with signature potpourri will not break the bank. Small silk-covered boxes and jewel cases, tassels, braids, pillows, picture frames, and photo albums are also available in a variety of colors and styles.

59

BRANDIMARTE

VIALE L. ARIOSTO 11c/R

▭ ☎ 055 23041 · *www.brandimarte.com*

MON-FRI 9AM-1PM & 2-7PM; SAT 9AM-1PM & 3-7PM

CLOSED SUNDAY

FOR OVER HALF A CENTURY, BRANDIMARTE HAS BEEN KNOWN FOR ITS DISTINCTIVE SIGNATURE hammered silver, in styles from classical to Deco to Modern. Artfully displayed in this spacious, gleaming showroom are handmade candlesticks, vases, bowls, goblets, kitchen utensils, tableware, napkin rings, picture frames, clocks, table lamps, trays, oversized jewelry, and desk sets. A silver pacifier or miniature table setting makes a memorable gift for a newborn, and the stylish spaghetti fork will make an impression on just about anyone.

The very helpful staff will ship worldwide.

60

STEFANO BEMER

BORGO SAN FREDIANO 143R

🚇 ☎ 055 222558 · *www.stefanobemer.it*

MON-SAT 9AM-1PM & 3:30-7:30PM

CLOSED SUNDAY & AUGUST

SINCE 1983, STEFANO BEMER, MAESTRO *CALZOLAIO*, HAS BEEN ATTENDING TO THE FEET OF THE Florentine elite. Working with two assistants in the back of his small shop on Borgo San Frediano, he creates exquisite butter-soft custom-made shoes for men. To place an order, two visits are required: first, to take measurements and to select style and materials. After two months is the first fitting; one month later, the shoes are ready. Once the wooden forms are made, a second pair of shoes will cost substantially less. If your feet are too impatient, a ready-to-wear line is available at Bemer's nearby showroom on Via Camaldoli 10r.

[174]

IL PARALUME

BORGO SAN FREDIANO 47

☎ 055 2396760 · *www.ilparalume.it*

MON-SAT 8:30AM-1PM & 3:30-7:30PM;

SAT 8:30AM-1PM; CLOSED SUNDAY

FOR DECADES, IL PARALUME HAS BEEN PRO-DUCING LAMPS AND LAMPSHADES OUT OF ITS labyrinthine workshop at the back of the store. Classic Florentine chandeliers, wall lamps, table lamps, tables, and mirrors are all made by hand, using only Italian materials. The hand-painted lamp bases are crafted from carved wood and metal, and are either left natural, gold plated, or lacquered.

Despite the hundreds of styles to choose from in both the workshop and showroom across the street, should you not find exactly what you are looking for, it can be created for you, which will take about a week's time.

TWISTED

BORGO SAN FREDIANO 21R

☎ 055 282011

MON-SAT 9AM-12:30PM & 3-7:30PM

CLOSED SUNDAY

STEFANO NUZZO'S FIVE-YEAR-OLD SHOP ON BORGO SAN FREDIANO IS A HAVEN FOR THE JAZZ ENTHU-siast. New and used CDs, videos, DVDs, scores, books, posters, and postcards address all things jazz, from early, hard-to-find recordings to up-to-the minute releases.

In his brightly lit, unadorned store, Nuzzo will let you preview your selection in a listening station before you make your purchase.

[177]

[178]

CERI VINTAGE

VIA DEI SERRAGLI 26R

🖅 ☎ 055 217978

MON-SAT 9:30AM-12:30PM, 3:30-7PM

CLOSED SUNDAY

Danilo Ceri started collecting military uniforms ten years ago, but today his spacious shop on Via Serragli includes clothing, accessories, costume jewelry, hats, boots, shoes, handbags, toys, posters, sewing patterns, and, of course, militaria, from the 1880s through the 1980s.

Housed in a fifteenth-century palazzo with soaring ceilings, his stock is replenished every five days, and is culled from sources all over the world.

The clothing, which is *"novanta per cento donna"* (90% for women), is in mint condition.

FRANCESCO DA FIRENZE

VIA SANTO SPIRITO 62R

☎ 055 212428

MON-SAT 9AM-1PM & 3:30-7:30PM

CLOSED SUNDAY

BEHIND THIS BLINK-AND-YOU'LL-MISS-IT STORE-FRONT YOU WILL DISCOVER THE WORKSHOP OF Francesco Laudato, the source for classic and comfortable handmade leather shoes, sandals, boots, *sambi* (mules), and loafers for both men and women. Choose from his in-store stock, or you can place a custom order: expect one month for a pair of shoes (which he can ship to you), and only a few days for sandals. Everything is made in the back of the shop by Francesco himself, who has been working at his craft since 1976.

A reasonably-priced selection of briefcases and wallets is also available.

[181]

65

CASTORINA

VIA SANTO SPIRITO 13/15R

📠 ☎ 055 212885 · *www.castorina.net*

MON-FRI 9AM-1PM & 3:30-7:30PM; SAT 9AM-1PM

CLOSED SUNDAY & AUGUST

THE CASTORINA FAMILY, OF SICILIAN ORIGIN, HAS BEEN A LEADER IN WOOD CARVING SINCE 1895. Their vast store is filled with an impressive array of moldings, columns, candlesticks, obelisks, trompe l'oeil tables, reading stands, mirrors and frames, angels and *putti*, goblets, vases, ornaments, fruit dishes and trays, globes, orbs, and lamp bases. All are available in a huge selection of woods, finishes, and inlay patterns. While the sheer volume may be daunting, many of the smaller carved decorative elements (which Florentines use for furniture repair) can make distinctive souvenirs.

[183]

66

STUDIO PUCK

VIA SANTO SPIRITO 28R

▭ ☎ 055 280954 · *www.studiopuck.it*

MON-FRI 9AM-7PM; SAT 9:30AM-1PM

CLOSED SUNDAY

A RELATIVE NEWCOMER (20 YEARS) TO THIS HISTORIC NEIGHBORHOOD OF ARTISAN WORK-shops, Studio Puck (pronounced *Pook*) takes crafts-manship to new heights. This staggeringly beautiful showroom features fine engravings that are printed on nineteenth-century presses, hand-colored with gouache and watercolors, and then matted and decorated by hand using Florentine marbled paper. They are finished using time-honored techniques in equally distinctive hand-polished frames of cherry, walnut, chestnut, gold leaf, or leather, and enhanced with elegant fabrics.

[186]

APROSIO & CO

VIA SANTO SPIRITO 11

☎ 055 290534 · *www.aprosio.it*

MON-SAT 9:30AM-1PM & 3:30-7:30PM

CLOSED SUNDAY

HOUSED IN THE HISTORIC THIRTEENTH-CENTURY PALAZZO FRESCOBALDI, THIS UNFORGETTABLE store showcases Ornella Aprosio's breathtaking designs of delicately woven glass jewelry and accessories.

A team of experienced artisans works with minute glass beads and crystals, from Venice and the Czech Republic, respectively, to create exquisite earrings, bracelets, necklaces, brooches, purses, gloves, and hats. Aprosio, who draws her inspiration from nature, uses themes of flowers, fruits, insects, and the sea, offering a contemporary interpretation of an ancient craft.

OLIO & CONVIVIUM

68

VIA SANTO SPIRITO 4

☎ 055 2658198 · *www.conviviumfirenze.it*

MON 10AM-3PM; TUE-SAT 10AM-3PM & 5:30-10:30PM

CLOSED SUNDAY

THE TILED FLOORS AND SPARKLING INTERIOR OF OLIO & CONVIVIUM PROVIDE A LOVELY RESPITE along this street of workshops. Tuscan specialties of every variety are offered in this cheerful "gastronomic atelier," featuring artisan breads, pastas, *salumi*, cheeses, and of course excellent extra virgin olive oils. The *oleoteca didattica* (oil tasting room) will turn anyone into a sated connoisseur. Cooking classes are given in the airy, open kitchen, and wine tasting seminars are held in the atelier.

The small adjacent restaurant is a perfect spot for a quick and satisfying lunch or wine tasting.

WALK 7 ✦ FOOD & DRINK

TRATTORIA DEL CARMINE

(c) *Piazza del Carmine 18r* 🚋 ☎ 055 218601
Lunch and dinner daily · Inexpensive/Moderate

An institution for fifty years, this warm and welcoming family restaurant serves traditional Tuscan fare such as *bistecca fiorentina* (which the chef will bring to your table for your approval before grilling it) and fresh porcini mushrooms, in a no-nonsense decor, at reasonable prices. Good for people-watching, especially in warmer weather when outdoor seating is available.

CAVOLO NERO

(d) *Via d'Ardiglione 22* 🚋 ☎ 055 294744 · *www.cavolonero.it*
Dinner daily · Moderate/Expensive

Michela and Arturo Dori's elegant restaurant serves sophisticated Mediterranean cuisine in an intimate, modern setting. Start off with Cavolo Nero's unique selection of breads, flavored with tomato, squid ink, or olive, and move on to an innovative menu of pastas and main courses. Save room for Michela's remarkable *tenerina di cioccolata fondente* (warm chocolate tart). In summer, the charming jasmine-filled garden will add to your dining enjoyment.

IL SANTO BEVITORE
Via Santo Spirito 64/66r 📠 ☎ 055 211264
www.ilsantobevitore.com
Lunch Mon-Fri, Dinner Mon-Sat
Closed Sunday · Moderate

In this spacious, bright room with Renaissance vaulted ceilings, the creative, carefully selected lunch menu changes daily, offering soups, pastas, and salads. Try the perfectly *al dente* spaghetti with mussels, sea bass, and cherry tomatoes, or the cream of garbanzo bean soup doused with rosemary oil. The dinner menu changes with the season. More than 15 different wines are offered by the glass, as well as a tasting menu of wine, vin santos, and grappas.

OLIO & CONVIVIUM
Via Santo Spirito 4 📠 ☎ 055 2658198
www.conviviumfirenze.it
Mon 10am-3pm; Tue-Sat 10am-3pm, 5:30-10:30pm; Closed Sunday
(see shop 68, p. 188)

A lovely spot for lunch, dinner, or an *aperitivo*. Excellent wines by the glass, as well as cheeses, *salumi*, and oil tastings, are offered by a knowledgeable staff. Choose the the right-hand room as you enter, where you can watch the chefs busily at work in the kitchen.

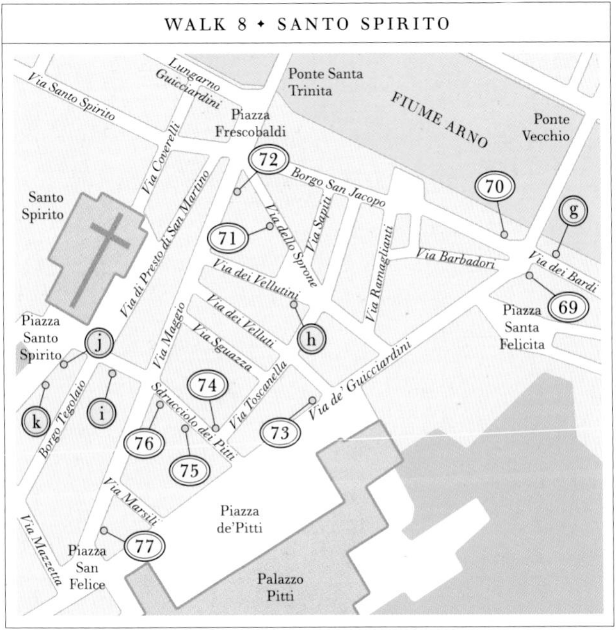
WALK 8 ✦ SANTO SPIRITO
Lungarno Guicciardini
Via Santo Spirito
Ponte Santa Trinita
FIUME ARNO
Ponte Vecchio
Piazza Frescobaldi
Via Coverelli
72
Borgo San Jacopo
70
g
Santo Spirito
Via di Presto di San Martino
71
Via dello Sprone
Via Sapiti
Via Ramaglianti
Via Barbadori
Via dei Bardi
Via dei Vellutini
69
Piazza Santa Felicita
Piazza Santo Spirito
j
Via Maggio
Via dei Velluti
h
Via Sguazza
Via Toscanella
Via de' Guicciardini
74
73
k
i
Borgo Tegolaio
76
Sdrucciolo dei Pitti
75
Via Marsili
Piazza de'Pitti
Via Mazzetta
Piazza San Felice
77
Palazzo Pitti

SHOPS

69 Madova

70 Beatrice Galli

71 Giuditta Blandini

72 Bartolozzi e Maioli

73 Giulio Giannini & Figlio

74 Geraldine Tayar

75 Le Telerie Toscane

76 Pitti Vintage

77 Dolcissimo

FOOD & DRINK

g Golden View Open Bar

h Trattoria 4 Leoni

i Trattoria La Casalinga

j Borgo Antico

k Caffè Ricchi

MADOVA

VIA DE' GUICCIARDINI 1R

▭ ☎ 055 2396526 · *www.madova.com*

MON-SAT 9:30AM-7:30PM

CLOSED SUNDAY

I N FLORENCE, *GUANTI* (GLOVES) ARE SYNONYMOUS WITH MADOVA, SPECIALISTS IN THE FIELD SINCE 1919. Proud to be the only shop in Europe that produces and sells leather gloves exclusively (made in its factory just steps from the shop), these butter-soft gloves come in a spectrum of beautiful colors, with linings of silk, lambswool, or leather.

Simply walk into the shop and present your hand, and Madova will do the rest. Without even having to measure, the expert staff will not only know what size you are, but what type of leather, in what color, will go best with what you're wearing. And they're always right.

[195]

70

BEATRICE GALLI

BORGO SAN JACOPO 24R

▭ ☎ 055 289193

MON-SAT 9:30AM-1PM & 2-6PM

CLOSED SUNDAY

BEATRICE GALLI'S ENTHUSIASM FOR KNITTING IS INFECTIOUS. (SHE GOT HER START AT THE AGE of six.) With a spectacular view of the Arno, her long, narrow shop hosts an extraordinary selection of beautifully colored yarns, all made in Italy. *Fettuccine di seta*, subtly hued ribbons of silk, are irresistible, as are any of the offerings of cashmere, merino, alpaca, and angora.

Once you become part of her loyal clientele, Signora Galli will gladly send additional skeins as needed.

If you happen to fall in love with the yarns but are all thumbs, exquisite shawls and scarves, handwoven by Galli, are also available, as are hand-crocheted hats.

[197]

GIUDITTA BLANDINI

VIA DELLO SPRONE 25R

▬ ☎ 055 2776275 · *www.stilebiologico.it*

MON 3:30-7:30PM; TUE-SAT 9AM-1PM & 3:30-7:30PM

CLOSED SUNDAY

A LEADER IN ENVIRONMENTALLY CONSCIOUS FASHION, GIUDITTA BLANDINI DESIGNS HER own line of beautiful and sophisticated clothing in *stile biologico*—using natural fibers that have not been chemically treated. Since 1997, her eponymous shop on Via dello Sprone has featured simple and elegant sweaters, dresses, skirts, blouses, shawls, bags, and children's clothes in lovely muted colors.

These exceedingly comfortable yet stylish creations are fabricated in Tuscany from untreated raw silk, hemp, alpaca, and lambswool, and organic cotton and linen, using only vegetable dyes.

BARTOLOZZI E MAIOLI

VIA MAGGIO 13R

✆ 055 2398633 · *www.bartolozzi.net*

MON-SAT 9AM-1PM & 3:30-7PM

CLOSED SUNDAY & AUGUST

SINCE 1936, FIORENZO BARTOLOZZI'S WOOD CARV-ING ARTISTRY HAS BEEN LEGENDARY, PARTICU-larly his restoration of the choir benches in the Abbey of Montecassino after it was destroyed during World War II. Now under the direction of his daughter, Fiorenza, this workshop/showroom is replete with anything and everything carved and gilded, large and small. The store offers a mesmerizing and seemingly endless display of beautifully sculpted picture frames, candelabras, cherubs, and other *objets*, while at a table in the back, artisans are quietly at work on still more creations.

[201]

73

GIULIO GIANNINI & FIGLIO

PIAZZA DE' PITTI 37R

▭ ☎ 055 212621

MON-SAT 10AM-7:30PM; SUN 10:30AM-6:30PM

SINCE 1856, GIULIO GIANNINI & FIGLIO HAS BEEN A FAVORITE FOR THEIR HANDMADE, QUINTES-sentially Florentine papers. Located directly across the street from the Pitti Palace, the shop carries blank books, journals, address books, stationery, cards, paper-wrapped pencils, bookplates, and frames, all in Giannini's distinctive patterns, and all made in Florence.

Tiny books labeled *"Oggetti dati in prestito"* (Things Loaned) or *Compleanni* (Birthdays) are also available in English and make charming gifts.

Free tours of the workshop are available; you will need to book one week in advance.

[203]

[204]

GERALDINE TAYAR

SDRUCCIOLO DEI PITTI 6R

☎ 055 290405

MON-SAT 9AM-1PM & 3-7PM

CLOSED SUNDAY

THE AFFABLE GERALDINE TAYAR SEEKS OUT UNUSUAL FABRICS TO DESIGN DELIGHTFUL clothes and accessories for women and children. Choose from the display rack of dresses, skirts, tops, handbags, belts, shawls, hats, and scarves, and within seven to ten days you will have your very own Tayar original.

Known to add to her repertoire as her family grows, Tayar first expanded into children's clothes, and more recently introduced a line of stylish dog collars, which are coordinated to match her ensembles. A favorite pet's name emblazoned in rhinestones, or trimmed in velvet, makes an unforgettable gift.

LE TELERIE TOSCANE

SDRUCCIOLO DEI PITTI 15R

▭ ☎ 055 216177

MON-FRI 10AM-1:30PM & 2:30-7PM

CLOSED SATURDAY & SUNDAY

TUCKED AWAY ON THIS TINY STREET THAT LEADS TO THE PITTI PALACE, LE TELERIE Toscane features traditional Tuscan table linens, including tablecloths, runners, placemats, and napkins, as well as bedsheets, duvet covers, coverlets, aprons, and dishcloths, all in exquisite printed and jacquard fabrics. Their exclusive designs include classic country motifs: hunting scenes, fruit baskets, and grapevines. One of the patterns is a replica of the tablecloth in Andrea del Castelagno's *Last Supper*, painted in 1450, at the Cenacolo of St. Apollonia. If your table or bed is a nontraditional size, they will be happy to design to fit, and will ship it to you.

[208]

PITTI VINTAGE

SDRUCCIOLO DEI PITTI 19R

📠 ☎ 055 2302676 · *www.pittivintage.it*

MON 3-7PM; TUE-SAT 10AM-2PM & 3-7PM

CLOSED SUNDAY

GRACIELA AVENDANO, A MEXICAN, AND LUIGI CAPETO, FROM APULIA, MET IN THE EAST VILLAGE of New York and decided to open a vintage clothing shop in Florence. Their vaulted space, with a hot pink room for women and an acid green one for men, carries a lively mix of clothes and accessories from the late 1800s to the late 1900s, all exclusively Italian. Labels such as Ferragamo, Fendi, Gucci, and Prada, in mint condition, are well represented. A vast selection of high-heeled shoes is in itself a grand tour of Italian fashion history.

In her workshop downstairs, Graciela designs her own line of unique vintage-inspired fashions.

DOLCISSIMO

VIA MAGGIO 61R

☎ 055 2396268 · *www.caffeitaliano.it*

TUE-SAT 9AM-1PM & 3:30-7:30PM;

SUN 9AM-1PM

THIS GLEAMING WHITE *LABORATORIO DI PASTIC-CERIA* LINED WITH CANDY-FILLED APOTHECARY jars beckons to all passersby on Via Maggio. In the aptly-named Dolcissimo, a crystal chandelier hovers gracefully over elegant glass cases of *torte* and *biscotti* that are almost too beautiful to eat. (But you must—the *torta di cioccolato fondente e peperoncino* and the custard and fresh fruit tarts are superb.)

Part of the Caffè Italiano empire (see pages 44 and 134), Dolcissimo carries the parent company's signature coffee, as well as a line of their own fine chocolates, Sicilian *marmellate*, liqueurs, and grappas.

[211]

GOLDEN VIEW OPEN BAR

(g) *Via dei Bardi 58r* ▭ ☎ 055 214502

12 noon-12 midnight daily; pizza served until 1 am · Moderate

Despite the curious name, Golden View Open Bar's airy rooms looking out onto the Arno make it an excellent spot for lunch, *aperitivo*, or dinner. Beautifully presented antipasti, salads, pizzas, and main courses are served by a friendly staff just steps from the Ponte Vecchio. When calling for a reservation, be sure to ask for a table overlooking the river.

TRATTORIA 4 LEONI

(h) *Via dei Vellutini 1r* ▭ ☎ 055 218562

Lunch & dinner daily, closed Wednesday lunch · Moderate

Trattoria 4 Leoni is the essential Tuscan kitchen, appealing to local artisans and movie stars alike. Try the *gran fritto dell'aia* (fried barnyard)—chicken, rabbit, zucchini, eggplant, potatoes, and polenta served on rustic *carta paglia*. *Fiocchetti*, little "purses" of fresh pasta filled with asparagus and taleggio cheese, are not to be missed. The deceptively simple *insalata della Passera* (cabbage, zucchini, avocado, *pignoli*) is also quite satisfying. In spring and summer, savor your meal outside in the tiny Piazza della Passera.

TRATTORIA LA CASALINGA

Via dei Michelozzi 9r 🔲 ☎ 055 218624

Lunch & dinner, closed Sunday and 3 weeks in August · Inexpensive

La Casalinga, or The Housewife, says it all—simple, satisfying homestyle cooking, with a menu that changes daily, in a boisterous setting. Prices are astonishingly reasonable.

BORGO ANTICO

Piazza Santo Spirito 6r 🔲 ☎ 055 210437

Lunch & dinner, closed Monday · Moderate

Borgo Antico is a good choice for an alfresco lunch or dinner on the Piazza Santo Spirito, where regulars like to come for excellent pizzas, risottos, and salads.

CAFFÈ RICCHI

Piazza Santo Spirito 9r 🔲 ☎ 055 282173 ⓚ

Lunch & dinner, closed Sunday · Moderate

Delicious pastas, pizzas, and composed salads at reasonable prices make Ricchi an ideal lunch spot, particularly in good weather, when you can sit outdoors and enjoy the quiet charm of Piazza Santo Spirito. Next door at number 8r is their restaurant, which is only open for dinner, and pricier.

AUTHOR'S FAVORITES

INDEX BY SPECIALTY

[216]

[218]

ALPHABETICAL INDEX

ACKNOWLEDGEMENTS

I would like to thank Angela Hederman of the Little Bookroom for encouraging me to write this book.

In Florence, my deepest gratitude to my friend and advisor Lise Apatoff, without whose expert guidance this book could never have happened; Jackie Roberts for so many memorable restaurant adventures; Mariangela Catalani of Le Stanze di Santa Croce for her fine accommodations and recommendations; Sandra Dori and Cinzia Calamai for their hospitality; Alessandra and Donatella Ragionieri; Marica Corsi; and of course all of the shops and restaurants who graciously took time from their busy schedules to be interviewed.

In New York, I am indebted to my staff, Chad Roberts and Jennifer Blanco, for bringing this book to a reality, and Rosella Matt for her expertise. And finally, to my family, Steven and Nicolas Heller, for their love, patience, and support. *Mille grazie a tutti.*

ABOUT THE AUTHOR

LOUISE FILI, a lifelong Italophile, is principal of Louise Fili Ltd, a New York City graphic design firm specializing in logos, food packaging, and restaurant identities. For over a decade, she was art director of Pantheon Books, where she designed over 2000 book jackets. Fili has designed and co-authored, with Steven Heller, *Italian Art Deco*, *Dutch Moderne*, *Streamline*, *British Modern*, *Deco España*, *German Modern*, *Deco Type*, *French Modern*, *Cover Story*, *Design Connoisseur*, *Counter Culture*, *Typology*, and *Stylepedia*. Her work is in the permanent collections of the Library of Congress, the Cooper Hewitt Museum, the Bibliothèque Nationale and the Musée des Arts Decoratifs. In 2004 she was inducted into the Art Directors Hall of Fame.